D0120559

NOT A WAVE VISIBLE
AND OTHER PLAYS

NOT A WAVE VISIBLE AND OTHER PLAYS

DOMINIC O'SULLIVAN

To order additional copies of this book, contact:
Xlibris Corporation
1-888-795-4274
www.Xlibris.com
Orders@Xlibris.com
300797

CONTENTS

MR. K'S HOUSE

CAST LIST

Adam

Man

Woman

Librarian

Robert—A lawyer

Anna—Robert's wife

Miriam—Anna's sister

Warder

E

First Man

Second Man

Two Workmen

SCENE 1

(A deserted street. One or two leaves are blown down it. Adam approaches. He appears to be looking for something. There is a Man at the end of the street. They cross in the middle. They exchange glances. They pass. Adam goes a couple of steps back)

ADAM: Excuse me?

MAN: *(Pretends not to hear)*

ADAM: Excuse me?

MAN: *(Turns round)* Yes?

ADAM: I wonder if you could help me.

MAN: Me?

ADAM: There's no one *else* about.

MAN: Yes.

ADAM: Can you tell me where the library is?

MAN: Ah, the library.

ADAM: Yes.

MAN: The library, you said?

ADAM: Yes.

MAN: Hmm. Now let me think. When I last saw it, it was on Joseph Square.

ADAM: When you *last* saw it?

MAN: Yes.

ADAM: Seems strange. Does it move around? Is it a mobile library?

MAN: In a manner of speaking.

ADAM: I'm glad I asked, then.

MAN: Yes. Yes, you're right. You did well to ask but I'm not sure I'm the right person to help you. Look! There's someone at the end of the street. Let's ask them if they know.

WOMAN: Good day, gentlemen.

MAN: My, er . . . this gentleman is looking for the library.

WOMAN: The library? Now there's a thing. You don't often get asked for the library. The bakery, yes, and the Golden Lion. They do a good drop of beer in there, by the way. Are you sure you wouldn't like the Golden Lion? Nice wooden benches. Bit hard on your arse, mind. I always takes a cushion. Pleasant company, lovely soups. I can tell you where *that* is.

MAN: Well, so could I.

MAN and WOMAN: We could *both* tell you.

ADAM: I was looking for the library, actually. You see, I need a book.

MAN and WOMAN: (*Surprised*) A book?

ADAM: Or rather I want to look something up.

WOMAN: You're not a detective, are you? I read that Sherlock Holmes once. Quite good it was. Funny address, though. You're not Sherlock Holmes, are you?

ADAM: (*Smiling*) No, I'm not Sherlock Holmes.

MAN: Madam, I don't think you should be reading those kinds of books. We have writers much closer to home.

WOMAN:	Do we? I've never seen any. Are they out on the streets? Anyway, I enjoyed my Sherlock Holmes and his Doctor Wotsit.
MAN:	I feel it's hardly a good influence, though. A drug addict *and* a homosexual.
WOMAN:	A pansy? I must have missed that. He played such a lovely violin, too. Anyway, how come *you* know so much about it?
MAN:	One has to read so as to be able to argue from a position of strength. To dispute from ignorance would be mere folly.
WOMAN:	(*Scornful*) Ooh! Hark at him!
MAN:	But as I said, it's not something to be encouraged. I mean, what kind of example is that to set to young minds? (*They both turn to Adam*)
WOMAN:	Can we help you, young man? You seem very interested in our conversation.
ADAM:	No, no. I was merely listening. It would have been rude to walk away.
MAN:	Eavesdropping, more like. Here am I having a literary discussion . . .
WOMAN:	Ssh! Don't say it too loud. There may be a window opening.
MAN:	I'm sorry. (*To Adam*) Well?
ADAM:	I'm still looking for the library. (*Man and Woman look at each other*)
MAN:	Oh yes, of course. Of course you are.
ADAM:	I mean I haven't given up. And I was *hardly* eavesdropping.
MAN:	Take no notice. Just over-reacting.
WOMAN:	It's the time of day.
MAN:	Our mistake. (*Thinking*) Now, the library . . .

ADAM: Yes. You said something about it being in Joseph Square.

MAN: Yes, it was. At least it was when *I* last saw it.

WOMAN: Moves around, dear. One week it was in the High Street.

ADAM: One week!

WOMAN: That's right.

MAN: It's rather a versatile library. Not your typical, average . . .

ADAM: But it's no longer in the High Street?

WOMAN: I said was, didn't I? Past tense, you know.

MAN: Ssh! Don't say that word too loud.

WOMAN: Sorry, dear. I forget meself sometimes.

MAN: So I see.

WOMAN: Pity, 'cos I liked the library in the High Street. It was really quite convenient. I used to pop in for a wee after I'd bought me fish. Trouble was that woman at the counter. Right snotty, she was. Got a nose like a sheep. She would always smell the fish and order me out. No fish in the library, she says.

MAN: Well, there's a nonsense. What about those guppies?

WOMAN: Who said anything about a Labrador? No, it's against the rules, she said. We're not an eatery or a snack bar. The funny thing was, I had a look at the rules the next day and there was *nothing* about fish in the library.

MAN: I think it's outrageous. It just goes to show. You give someone a position of power and they abuse it.

WOMAN: I think it's those spectacles she wears on a chain round her neck.

MAN: You think so?

WOMAN:	It made her more cantankerous. It happened to my uncle. It's a well known fact.
MAN:	Made her more severe, I expect.
ADAM:	(*Coughs*) I don't wish to appear rude and I don't want to walk off again, but what about the library?
WOMAN:	Oh yes, now we're coming to that.
MAN:	The impetuousness of youth!
WOMAN:	(*Narked*) Honestly, some people have no patience. After all, it's not an easy thing you asked for. Now if it had been a bank . . .
ADAM:	But I don't want a bank.
MAN:	He doesn't want a bank. He's got no money.
ADAM:	How do you know I've got no money?
MAN:	Well it's obvious. Just looking at you. I can tell . . .
ADAM:	Oh you *can*, can you? What *else* can you tell?
WOMAN:	(*Laughing*) I can tell that he's not from round here.
ADAM:	Oh yes?
WOMAN:	Otherwise he wouldn't be asking for the library. (*Laughs*)
ADAM:	Most astute, I can see. It's all those detective novels you've been reading.
WOMAN:	Thank you, dear.
MAN:	I said we weren't to mention them!
ADAM:	Er, the library. Could we mention *that*, please? Or perhaps I should ask somebody else.
MAN:	There is nobody else.
ADAM:	How do you know?

MAN: They've all got memories like goldfishes.

ADAM: But how do you know?

MAN: Well, can you *see* anyone else?

ADAM: No, not at present. But I'm sure I might bump into someone.

WOMAN: Then you should look where you're going, sonny. (*Laughs*)

ADAM: Pardon?

WOMAN: You heard.

ADAM: Well, thank you. I can see I'm taking up far too much of your valuable time.

MAN: No, no. I'm in no hurry.

WOMAN: Me neither.

ADAM: So I see.

WOMAN: We'll try and trace the library for you.

MAN: Yes. Now after Joseph Square . . .

WOMAN: And the High Street. (*Sighs*) I *did* like it there.

MAN: There was Roderick Grove . . .

WOMAN: And New Court Avenue . . .

MAN: Heroes Park.

WOMAN: And Rampant Horse Street. That was my favourite place to put a library.

MAN: What a name! So evocative. You can almost picture it. But I agree. I was sorry it moved. It was most splendid.

ADAM: If you don't mind me asking, but *why* does the library move around so much?

MAN: (*Astonished*) You ask a question like *that*!

ADAM: I did.

MAN:	An intelligent chap like yourself.
ADAM:	It wasn't in the past tense.
MAN:	We must be thankful for small mercies.
ADAM:	Just the present simple.
WOMAN:	I like it when it's simple.
ADAM:	Although, in reality, the present simple is perhaps far from simple. It has its roots in the past and affects the future.
MAN:	That's easy for you to say.
WOMAN:	Sounds lovely, though, doesn't it? The present future. *(Sighs)*
ADAM:	I was asking why the library moved around so much.
WOMAN:	Well, it's obvious, isn't it?
ADAM:	Is it some kind of mobile library, then?
MAN:	Uncultivated youth! Of course it moves. It's to bring it closer to the people that's why! To enable wider access. You don't need to go to the library. One day it'll come to you . . . or somewhere near you.
ADAM:	But why not have a mobile one?
MAN:	It wouldn't be the same.
WOMAN:	Mind you, it was so convenient in the High Street. Especially if you're having trouble with your waterworks.
ADAM:	But it must cost a fortune to keep moving it around.
MAN:	Accessibility is the name of the game. The new watchword.
ADAM:	Well how can it be accessible if no one knows where it is? You said so yourselves.
MAN:	We're still thinking.
WOMAN:	We're *trying* to help you.
ADAM:	I'm sorry.

MAN: The petulance of youth.

ADAM: I *said* I'm sorry.

MAN: Well, yes.

ADAM: Tell me, do they have many books in the library?

MAN: Books? Er . . .

WOMAN: No, not many. Just the usual favourites.

MAN: There were five the last time I went.

ADAM: Five!

WOMAN: They must have got a new one in.

MAN: That's the annual budget gone, then.

ADAM: But surely, if they moved less, they'd have more money to purchase books?

MAN: What about the accessibility, though? You'd lose that, wouldn't you?

ADAM: But what's the point of accessibility? From what you tell me, there's very little in the library to access.

MAN: It's easy to pick holes in an argument.

WOMAN: Yes, cleverclogs. Especially if you're not from round here.

MAN: It's the principle, after all, that has to be adhered to.

ADAM: But it's ridiculous to spend all that money on moving. It's such a waste.

WOMAN: Says you!

ADAM: I remember once, back in my city, I went down to the Education Office to hand in a petition. In the plush foyer they had carpets and palm trees and piped music.

WOMAN: Music! How romantic! What were they playing?

ADAM: I think you've missed the point.

WOMAN: No, I haven't. What were they playing?

ADAM: Engelbert Humperdinck, I think.

WOMAN: What a beautiful name! I wish I was called that. Sort of rolls off the tongue.

ADAM: And yet there were no chalk and dusters in the classrooms.

WOMAN: Classrooms? What have *they* got to do with it? I thought you were down at the offices. You wouldn't have classrooms there.

MAN: Was not were, sonny. Get your priorities right.

ADAM: It's a slip of the tongue, I'm sure.

MAN: Slips can be costly. Exercise caution.

WOMAN: Well I think it's a good thing to . . .

MAN: Project the right image.

WOMAN: Quite so.

MAN: I mean, why shouldn't the Education Department be nice? Makes you want to go in there all the more often. Don't you think so?

WOMAN: I agree. I'd certainly want to go in there. Mainly for the music and that beautiful name. Now what was it again?

ADAM: I'm close to despair.

WOMAN: No, it wasn't that.

MAN: What! How can you say that? Now come on, lad.

WOMAN: Yes.

MAN: Yes. We'll find you your library.

WOMAN: We will.

MAN: We'll make a concerted effort. Look, you stay with me and er . . .

WOMAN: Vera. That's me.

MAN: Will look in that direction. She's going up the street now and
            we'll look down it. *(He winks at her)* Is that all right? I mean,
            it's the *least* we can do.

ADAM: Yes. Thank you. You're very kind. And I'm sorry if I seemed
            ungrateful earlier.

MAN: Forgotten, isn't it, Ethel?

WOMAN: Vera.

MAN: Ethelvera. Now come on, you walk with me and I guarantee
            we'll come up with something. What exactly was it you wanted
            to find in the library?

            A book?

ADAM: Yes, possibly, but not just that. A library's an important
            information point, you know.

MAN: Don't we know it!

WOMAN: A pillow of the community.

MAN: You mean pillar, dear.

WOMAN: It *is* pillow. I'm not wrong. Some of my best friends go to sleep
            in the library in the winter months. It saves a fortune on the
            heating bills.

MAN: *(Looks up)* I thought I saw a snowflake just now.

WOMAN: Then they'll all be heading off like a shot. Very comfy some
            of those armchairs are there. Not the ones next to the window
            but the ones in the reference library. At nine o'clock there used
            to be a huge queue outside, just waiting for it to open.

MAN: *(Laughs)* So look out for long queues, then.

WOMAN: Silly! It'll be open now, so they'll all be safely tucked up inside. Who needs lots of books when you have plenty of comfy chairs you can go to sleep in? I ask you!

(Adam leaves with the Man. The Woman scuttles off. The stage is empty for a moment. A couple of workmen run on with a sign. In big letters it says Library. They quickly put up the sign)

(Lady Librarian, looking very similar to the Woman, takes up residence)

LIBRARIAN: Thank you, boys.

TWO WORKMEN: Thank you, madam.

LIBRARIAN *(Sighs)* So polite always. It's much appreciated.

(Adam and the Man walk up and down the streets searching quickly, almost frantically)

MAN: *(Pointing)* There you are. What did I tell you?

ADAM: What?

MAN: Look straight ahead, my boy. Your goal. Your ultimate quest.

(Voice off-stage: Was ever library serenaded thus?)

ADAM: So it is. *(Shakes the Man's hand)* I'm indebted to you. Thank you. Thank you, very much.

MAN: It takes a knack to make libraries happen, but think nothing of it. You'll be all right now, won't you?

ADAM: Yes, yes, of course.

MAN: Because I must rush home for my tea.

ADAM: Really? Well, I'm sorry to have kept you. And many thanks
               again.

MAN: Don't mention it.

ADAM: And I'm sorry if I was a little impatient earlier.

MAN: No, no. I won't hear of it. I was young once, you know. Ha,
               ha!

ADAM: Thanks again.

MAN: Goodbye.

ADAM: Goodbye to you. *(Enters library. There is a sound of heavy
               snoring. Adam walks to the library desk. The Librarian is painting
               her nails)*

LIBRARIAN: Won't be a minute.

ADAM: Okay. Yes.

LIBRARIAN: *(Takes a minute to finish painting. Adam looks round)* Now,
               there we are. I like to look nice for my customers.

ADAM: Yes, well, I was wondering if you could help me?

LIBRARIAN: I shall *try*. I mean, that's what we're here for. To help the public.
               (Snoring increases a little. She looks round) Provide assistance.
               Invaluable service.

ADAM: Yes, yes.

LIBRARIAN: So?

ADAM: Yes?

LIBRARIAN: What can I do for you?

ADAM: I'm looking for Franz's house.

LIBRARIAN: Is that Fran with a ce or a tz or a z?

ADAM: With a z.

LIBRARIAN: That'll be Mr. K, then?

ADAM: The very one.

LIBRARIAN: Hold on a minute. I'm not quite sure. I'll have to ask. *(Calling)* Martin! Are you there? Got a gentleman here looking for Mr. Franz's house.

(She leaves) I'll be back in a moment.

(Adam strolls around for a few minutes)

LIBRARIAN: *(Returns. Sniffs)* That's funny. I thought I could smell fish here.

ADAM: Never touch the stuff.

LIBRARIAN: Just as well. Now Martin says that it was on Castle Hill but thinks it might have moved since.

ADAM: Moved? I don't believe it! It's taken me all this time to get here! Everything keeps moving!

LIBRARIAN: Well, I'm only giving you the information. There's no need to shout.

ADAM: I wasn't.

LIBRARIAN: And if you're going to be stroppy with me, I'm going to have to ask you to leave the library. As it is, there's a terrible smell of fish here and we don't allow . . .

ADAM: *(Despairingly)* If you don't mind, I 'm going to have to sit down for a minute. It's been a long afternoon.

LIBRARIAN: *(Grudgingly)* Feel free.

ADAM: I must have walked miles.

LIBRARIAN: You'll find the armchairs by the window are the most comfy.

ADAM: Really? Thank you.

LIBRARIAN: We'll call you if we come up with anything.

ADAM: Thanks.

LIBRARIAN: Now you just sit back and relax. Take your mind off things.

(There is a great explosion outside. Of rubble falling, of stones tumbling, of a wall falling)

SCENE 2

(A spartan but tastefully furnished room in Robert and Anna's flat.)

ANNA: You're very quiet.

ROBERT: Am I?

ANNA: Yes, you are.

ROBERT: I'm sorry. *(Gets up. Walks around. Sits down)*

ANNA: What are you thinking about?

ROBERT: Thinking about? *(Laughs)* Funny that. You nearly always ask me.

ANNA: And *you* don't?

ROBERT: Yes.

ANNA: That's not true.

ROBERT: No?

ANNA: The aquarium.

ROBERT: The aquarium?

ANNA: Yes, the aquarium.

ROBERT: Ah.

ANNA: Had you forgotten? I was looking at the porcupine fish and you asked me.

ROBERT: I did?

ANNA: Who it looked like?

ROBERT: That's hardly the same.

ANNA: It is, because before that you asked me what I was thinking.

ROBERT: Did I?

ANNA: Yes, you did. And there was the time . . .

ROBERT: Okay, let's leave it, shall we?

ANNA: *(Surprised)* Okay, okay. *(Pause)* Why are you so tetchy today?

ROBERT: Am I?

ANNA: Yes, you are.

ROBERT: Just work, I suppose.

ANNA: You've never complained before.

ROBERT: There's always a first time.

ANNA: It's still unlike you.

ROBERT: Well, there you are, then.

ANNA: Are you going to tell me?

ROBERT: Tell you what? There's nothing really to tell. New client next Monday. Yes, starting next Monday.

ANNA: A welcome client or an unwelcome one?

ROBERT: In this case, the latter.

ANNA: Couldn't you have turned it down?

ROBERT: Maybe.

ANNA: Anyone we know?

ROBERT: Oh yes! Yes, I think so.

SCENE 3

(Miriam's flat)

MIRIAM: How are you feeling now?

ROBERT: Feeling?

MIRIAM: Yes. Anna said you were irritable last night.

ROBERT: She phoned to tell you that?

MIRIAM: Well you know how it is. She likes to phone most days.

ROBERT: I'm glad I was able to provide your conversation with some backbone. Some substance.

MIRIAM: I don't want to spend the little time we have arguing.

ROBERT: No, I know you don't. I'm sorry.

MIRIAM: So what's wrong?

ROBERT: *(Hesitates)* They've given me a case. A big one.

MIRIAM: And you don't want it?

ROBERT: Not particularly. I'm not sure anyone would.

MIRIAM: No? But it could be a feather in your cap.

ROBERT: I hardly think so. Defending the indefensible.

MIRIAM: Someone has to, as you're always telling me. It's called justice.

ROBERT: *(Angrily)* Since when did *he* ever recognise justice, the corrupt old bastard?

MIRIAM: So it's a he, then? Any more clues? Though I think I can guess. Well maybe you *should* go for it. It might give you valuable insights.

ROBERT: Oh yes?

MIRIAM: Yes.

ROBERT: Really?

MIRIAM: I'm just thinking of you.

ROBERT: And I'm thinking of you, too. *(They kiss)*

SCENE 4

(Inside a prison)

WARDER: Good morning, sir.

ROBERT: Morning. (*Shows his card*)

WARDER: Ah yes. You've come to see our distinguished guest.

ROBERT: I have indeed. How's he doing?

WARDER: Reading, complaining, writing.

ROBERT: Writing? What's he writing?

WARDER: His memoirs, I expect. Memoirs of a stonemason. Something like that. Wouldn't have thought anyone would be interested.

ROBERT: Ah, you never know. In a ghoulish kind of way. (*Bell rings*)

WARDER: He'll be ready now.

ROBERT: Good. Might as well start sometime.

WARDER: If you'd like to follow me. (*Various doors are locked and unlocked*)

ROBERT: I suppose it won't be an entirely new experience for him.

WARDER: How's that, sir?

ROBERT: From what I gather he was banged up in Cotttbus once.

WARDER: Is that right, sir? In *that* place? Well *you've* done your homework.

ROBERT: I'm sure he'll have done his. Still, you never know. It might come in useful sometime.

WARDER: *(Unlocking another door)* Here we are, sir. There'll be someone outside.

ROBERT: I hardly think that's necessary. He's not going to attack me or make a run for it.

WARDER: All the same, sir.

(They enter a dimly lit room. 'E' is sitting at a desk. He is writing vigorously)

ROBERT: Good day to you.

E: Oh yes.

            (He pauses for a moment. He carries on writing then puts down the pen)
            You'll forgive me if I don't get up.

ROBERT: There's nothing to forgive. (There is the sound of keys jangling outside)

E: (Turns round. Looks at him) Really? Is that so? Exonerated? And so soon! Well, we can all go home, then.

ROBERT: Hardly.

E: You know this is an illegal detention.

ROBERT: I doubt it.

E: Oh you doubt it, do you?

ROBERT: Not from the law books I'm looking at.

E: (Bangs the table) I insist on the right to be tried under our law. Our sovereign state.

ROBERT:	Excuse me, but where is that state? It's all but disappeared.
E:	That's a matter of opinion.
ROBERT:	And under which you'd no doubt be acquitted.
E:	It's possible.
ROBERT:	But our law is your law now. Yours. Our gift to you.
E:	It is an illegal occupation . . .
ROBERT:	Forgive me, but that seems a little rich coming from you.
E:	Perpetrated by fat West German bastards.
ROBERT:	(Laughs)
E:	I see that it amuses you.
ROBERT:	Just a little.
E:	But for the record, as Head of State . . .
ROBERT:	Former Head of State, surely? You resigned, didn't you? Dissolved yourself, or whatever it is you do.
E:	Only to comply with the wishes of the Party.
ROBERT:	And you yourself supported the motion.
E:	To further the interests of the Party. That was the important thing.
ROBERT:	Very magnanimous. I'm sure your people will cry out in gratitude.
E:	Maybe they will one day, but not for that. When they realise the mistake—and, forgive me, but you said 'your people'; I thought they were yours now.
ROBERT:	Yes. Yes, they are.
E:	I still demand to be tried under the laws of our country.
ROBERT:	More confusion now. Yours or ours?
E:	Of the People's Democratic Republic.

ROBERT: *(Laughs)* Democratic. That's a laugh. How can you *use* that word?

E: We had opposition parties. We observed the due process.

ROBERT: Parties with no teeth. Puppets. It's ludicrous.

E: I don't have all day for this. We're getting nowhere. Spare me this foolishness.

ROBERT: Now why does that seem familiar, too? Going nowhere?

E: (Angrily) Because nowhere is a lie!

SCENE 5

(The Library. Adam is dozing in one of the chairs.
Two men march in)

MAN 1:   Wake up please, sir.

ADAM: Pardon? What? Oh yes, I must have fallen asleep.

MAN 1:   We would ask you to leave, sir. please.

ADAM: Leave? Leave the library? But I haven't found what I was looking for.

MAN 2:   That's irrelevant.

ADAM: But that's why I came. Heaven knows it cost me an arm and a leg to get here.

MAN 2:   And it might cost you another if you don't. Leave, that is.

ADAM: Why should I leave?

MAN 1:   You've broken library rules, sir.

ADAM: What rules? Oh, the sleeping. Well, I apologise for that. Only it was so warm here and I'd been walking round the streets for so long trying to find the place . . .

MAN 1:   It's not the sleeping, although we wouldn't like you to make a habit of it.

MAN 2:   Some people come and park themselves here all day.

ADAM: Oh yes. The woman told me about it.

MAN 1:   Which woman? You mean the librarian?

ADAM: No, no. The woman who helped me to find this place. They went to a lot of trouble.

MAN 1:   They?

ADAM: There were two of them.

MAN 2:   Did they know each other?

ADAM: No, probably not. They helped me. Why all these questions?

MAN 1:   We need names.

ADAM: Names? Well, I'd never met them before.

MAN 2:   We'll look at the security cameras, seeing as you're unwilling to co-operate.

ADAM: How can I co-operate when I don't know them. I'd never met them before.

MAN 2:   Any friends, family, they mentioned.

ADAM: What is this? I just came here to get some information.

MAN 1:   What kind of information?

ADAM: I wanted to find the address of Mr. K's house.

MAN 1:   Mr. K?

ADAM: Yes. Do you know it?

MAN 1:   I may do.

ADAM: I wanted to visit the house.

MAN 2:   I think it's moved.

ADAM: That's what they said.

MAN 1:   Why do you want to go there?

ADAM: I want to see it. The house of a great artist.

MAN 2:   In your opinion.

MAN 1:   Too esoteric for me.

MAN 2:   Beyond the comprehension of most people.

MAN 1:   Elitist. (Second Man winces)

ADAM: And why does it keep being moved?

MAN 1:   We're not able to comment on that.

ADAM: And why does the library keep moving and yet have so few books?

MAN 1:   We're not here to answer questions.

MAN 2:   Please leave with us, sir. And don't make a scene.

ADAM: You said I'd broken library rules. What were they?

MAN 1:   I should have thought that was obvious, sir. You've been eating fish.

(They hurriedly escort him out)

SCENE 6

(Robert and Anna's flat)

MIRIAM: You seem tired, Anna.

ANNA: A little. It'll pass.

MIRIAM: Not sleeping?

ANNA: Enough. Well perhaps not. It'll pass.

MIRIAM: Outside my window the big black birds bark in the morning. So early.

ANNA: Crows. They'll be crows.

MIRIAM: Very likely. They look like nuns gathering for a convention.

ANNA: What a strange image! Where we are, no birds sing. I haven't heard the sound of birdsong in years.

MIRIAM: I wouldn't call this singing. *(Pause)* You're welcome to my crows. We can exchange them any time. Swap flats.

ANNA: I can't see Robert going for that, can you? A creature of habit. He likes his routine.

MIRIAM: Don't we all?

ANNA: Do we? *I* don't. I'd like a change.

MIRIAM: Change?

ANNA: Either that or go back to the way we were.

MIRIAM: *(Uneasily)* How do you mean?

ANNA: It's Robert. *(Sighs)* I don't know. He just seems different. Preoccupied. As if he were walking on a long rope greased with butter.

MIRIAM: Perhaps it's his work. You know what an important animal he is.

ANNA: You're calling my husband an animal?

MIRIAM: Aren't we all?

ANNA: Speak for yourself, Miriam.

MIRIAM: *(Laughs)* I bet he is at times. Especially after a long hard day in Court.

ANNA: Ha! *(Pause)* No, he seems . . . I don't know. Altered somehow. Not the same.

MIRIAM: We all change. Chameleons. Shedding our skin . . .

ANNA: I started wondering if he was seeing someone.

MIRIAM: *(Startled)* A doctor, you mean?

ANNA: No, no. Seeing someone.

MIRIAM: What makes you say that? You're happy, aren't you?

ANNA: Looking at him.

MIRIAM: Looking at him?

ANNA: Yes. And smelling him.

MIRIAM: What!

ANNA: Last week he smelt different. He smelt of someone else. Different . . . But just slightly familiar too. And there were subtle changes. Comings and goings. Different times. Different for a creature of routine.

MIRIAM: I see.

ANNA: And so . . .

MIRIAM: Yes?

ANNA: I began to smell a rat. Quite naturally.

SCENE 7

(The prison. E's cell)

E: (Looks up) Oh, it's you.

ROBERT: Spare me the rapturous welcome.

E: Back again so soon. Want another slanging match, then? More taunts?

ROBERT: I could hardly stay away.

E: That's what they all say. I'm beginning to feel like a zoo exhibit. Who knows, I'll wake up one morning and there'll be a collection box outside.

ROBERT: I daresay. Well, I'm glad you've retained a sense of humour. Mind you, an admission charge might not be such a bad idea. It might go some way to defray the costs of this expensive farce.

E: I'm glad you see it as a farce. Others would see it as some kind of showpiece. Still, it may not come to . . .

ROBERT: You could be right there. Not since 1945 has there been such a spectacular exhibition of . . .

E: I hope you're not comparing me with those . . .

ROBERT: I wouldn't dream of it.

E: And, anyway, you've got your dates wrong.

ROBERT: I make no comparisons. I was merely stating. Though I expect at that time even *you* were already calculating your ascent to the throne.

E: (Laughs) Ha! What's the weather like outside?

ROBERT: Why do you ask? Do you not have a window?

E: I have something that looks like a porthole.

ROBERT: So why not use it?

E: It's covered in filth.

ROBERT: Get them to clean it.

E: And my eyesight. It's not as good as it used to be. Besides, I've not been well.

ROBERT: But you can still see, can't you?

E: Has it been raining? That's all I want to know.

ROBERT: A little, yes.

E: What kind of rain?

ROBERT: What kind?

E: Yes. Damp, warm, chilly, clammy. In England they have all kinds of rain.

ROBERT: Do they? I've never been.

E: Neither have I, but I'm reliably informed.

ROBERT: That's good, then.

E: What is?

ROBERT: That you're reliably informed. As opposed to . . .

E: (Dismissively) Thank you.

ROBERT: I mean, far be it from me to interrupt the habits of a lifetime.

E: (Bangs his fist on the table) Always these little swipes! These jibes! Such insolence! Do you not realise whom you're speaking to?

ROBERT: Oh, I'm more than aware. I think you're imagining them. Confinement is making you sensitive. (Pause) Anyway, I was merely stating a point.

E: Were you?

ROBERT: Yes. Oh, by the way, the trial will be going ahead. There's been no change of plan.

E: Trial! A travesty! A pantomime! Done to assuage bourgeois respectabilities. Then they can say, look, we gave him a fair trial, that old bastard. That myopic little monster. But what a waste of money! Think how many flats and houses might have been built with that.

ROBERT: Your concern for the public purse is touching. But I doubt it.

E: Doubt what?

ROBERT: That they'll be saying that. There's very little interest. They've forgotten you already.

E: Impossible!

ROBERT: Oh yes. (Pause) Too bad, my friend. They've all wandered on to pastures new. They've left you standing in the rain. They've consigned you to the wastepaper basket of history.

E: Dustbin. (Long pause) But that's not possible. How can you forget forty years?

ROBERT: Easily.

E: Rain? (Pause) It's a temporary thing.

ROBERT: Once you make a hole in the dyke, water floods in. It washes over everything. There'll be no going back.

E: That's what you think. They'll soon see through you. And there's at least two generations who will remember what we did. Our achievements.

ROBERT: You make it sound like a partnership. And what achievements were those?

E: The care of the State for the citizen.

ROBERT: From the cradle to the grave? Oh yes. Well, excuse me if I don't sound very excited but I've heard it all before.

E: Unemployment did not exist. Everyone was provided for.

ROBERT: Well, yes, if you count frivolous jobs, I suppose. Little old men watching escalators; chambermaids on every hotel landing.

E: State benefits. Creches. Highest birth rate in Europe!

ROBERT: If you ask me, there wasn't much else to do over there but go forth and multiply.

E: And in your part, you had the lowest birth rate. How could that be? Answer me that.

ROBERT: I can't. You're right.

E: I'm so glad to have your acknowledgement.

ROBERT: But if everything was so rosy, why did they try to jump that wall you built?

E: Wall? That was no wall. It was a State Boundary.

ROBERT: It looked like a wall to me. Plenty of barbed wire and no chickens. A wall. It ran through people's houses, gardens, bedrooms even.

E: We have to draw a line somewhere.

ROBERT: It separated hearts and minds.

E: So what would you have done, then?

ROBERT: I wouldn't have built it.

E: No?

ROBERT: No.

E: Do you think we wanted it? (Pause) It was a measured reply to open provocation.

ROBERT: Oh yes? And what was that provocation? Freedom? Democracy? Choice? Oh, I'm sorry, you already said you were a democracy. One Unity Party firmly in command flanked by fawning, toothless oppositions. So fawning they were happy to be pissed on. No one, not even your own people believed that.

E: I'm surprised you're able to speak for my own people.

ROBERT: Someone had to.

E: And more surprised still that they chose you to represent me. They were really scraping the bottom of the barrel!

ROBERT: Listen, you toxic midget. There is no way that I represent you. I'm defending you, for want of a better word.

E: Well, if that's defence, heaven spare me an attack! And yet I feel we need to agree about this wall before we move on.

ROBERT: So it is a wall now? A few moments ago it was a State Boundary. What a transformation!

E: I'm humouring you in the spirit of compromise.

ROBERT: I'm not clutching my sides.

E: Pardon?

ROBERT: With mirth.

E: A slip of the tongue caused by duress.

ROBERT: You said you were humouring me.

E: Yes.

ROBERT: Nothing could put a calculating schemer like you under duress.

E: This feels like an interrogation to me.

ROBERT: If you wish it to be.

E: Don't you think I suffered qualms, too?

ROBERT: Pangs of conscience? Don't make me laugh!

E: So what would you have done, then?

ROBERT: I've never had to occupy the illustrious seat you appropriated.

E: Let's take an example, then. You might be more at home with that. A school . . . or a hospital, even. You take your children in before you go to work and there's nobody there. No staff, not even a receptionist. They're leaving in their droves. Doing a bunk. Running away.

ROBERT: It must have been your aftershave.

E: And a hospital, a clinic. Only there are no doctors, no nurses. The operating table lies empty. And no one to see to your children or the sick because they've all hopped on a tram to take them to the other side of town. And from there they cross through our country, on motorways, coaches and trains. And they take themselves off to the West. To fatter pay packets and more money.

ROBERT: They wanted what you couldn't give them. Despite all your five year plans and happy rallies, they wanted freedom. Fresh air. Real fresh air.

E: Everything is real.

ROBERT: (Laughs)

E: And what about the needs of State? The People? A country
            needs its workers, its skilled labourers. They are its lifeblood.
            Especially one that's trying to rebuild and reconstruct itself,
            with minimal help from anyone, after a period of unspeakable
            lunacy and deception. A country cannot afford, therefore,
            an exodus of self-seekers, or those who choose to shirk their
            responsibilities for individual gain and greed. If we had allowed
            it to go on, the country would have collapsed. We had to act.
            In the interests of all. Of everyone.

ROBERT: And foot trampled on heart to do so.

E: For the greater good. It had to be.

ROBERT: You had to act, you mean.

E: I wasn't in the forefront of things then, if you recall. I was
            merely a backroom boy.

ROBERT: That's a joke. The power behind the throne, more like. And it
            was only a matter of time before you toppled the incumbent.
            So don't give me that!

E: Renewal is the way forward. I've always been very clear about
            that. I even consented to my own removal. In fact I voted for it.

ROBERT: You hypocrite! You had no choice. You were all but out on
            your ear. They were baying for your blood.

E: (Looks at him for a moment. Robert is momentarily cowed)
            How dare you level the charge of hypocrisy against me! You'll
            not find me guilty of double standards.

ROBERT: What about the taking of the West's money? Your other half.
            You were happy to do that.

E: I took it for the right reasons.

ROBERT: Right reasons! Oh yes, and what were they?

E: To preserve Socialism.

ROBERT: Preserve Socialism?

E: And in that way the West was complicit. And if that's a crime, then guilty too.

ROBERT: You were blackmailing them.

E: They came to me.

ROBERT: Really?

E: They wanted it. A thaw in the proceedings. It was a feather to stick in their cap. It suited everyone.

ROBERT: Détente. A great word for nothing!

E: Okay, listen. You talk of freedom and democracy. So let me remind you of events back in Poland. 1979 to 1981.

ROBERT: Solidarnosc.

E: Precisely. And what was Solidarnosc? A trade union. A trade union which ultimately held the country to ransom. How you cheered and applauded from your seats in Parliament. Each strike receiving more and more approbation, more support. But what if Solidarity had been active in the West? Would it have been permitted to carry on, as it was, wrecking the machinery of State? Destroying the economy? Holding up vital supplies? No, I don't think so. So don't come the high and mighty with me about freedom because the thing is not everyone can afford it.

ROBERT:	You could have held your own rotten regime up in other ways. Did you never think to oil the wheels of change, however slight?
E:	There was the rapprochement of which I spoke.
ROBERT:	Only because you were broke.
E:	Far from it.
ROBERT:	You were wallowing in a mire of complacency. The clock was stopped.
E:	There wasn't a lot of choice, if you recall.
ROBERT:	I don't believe that! You don't mean to tell me your hands were completely tied.
E:	(Smiles) No. One hand was, the other wasn't. We always had to look over our shoulders, you know.
ROBERT:	Along with the rest of the population.
E:	Yes. Perhaps. And in that sense, I suppose, we were all equal.

SCENE 8

(Miriam's flat. The doorbell rings. Miriam goes to answer it. Robert enters.)

MIRIAM: Oh, it's you. I wasn't expecting you.

ROBERT: There's a warm welcome. Were you expecting someone else, then?

MIRIAM: *(Hesitantly)* No, no. I just didn't think you were coming.

ROBERT: I needed to see you.

MIRIAM: In what way *needed?*

ROBERT: Just needed.

MIRIAM: Sounds bad. Mind you, I'm not complaining. Hard day at the office?

ROBERT: You *could* say.

MIRIAM: Client proving difficult? Your big fish?

ROBERT: How do you know about that?

MIRIAM: Anna told me, of course. Said you were a bit on edge these days. Pressure of work and all that.

ROBERT: Yes.

MIRIAM: So is he?

ROBERT: Is he what?

MIRIAM: Proving difficult, your big fish?

ROBERT: The problem is he *still* thinks he's a big fish. He can't get his head round . . . But yes, he's prepared to argue.

MIRIAM: And what do you feel for him?

ROBERT: I try to feel nothing.

MIRIAM: Try?

ROBERT: Yes.

MIRIAM: But you *do* feel something?

ROBERT: Yes.

MIRIAM: What do you feel?

ROBERT: This is turning into an interrogation, Miriam.

MIRIAM: I asked you what you felt. I'm curious. I want to know, especially if it is who I think it is.

ROBERT: You *know?*

MIRIAM: Not for sure, no. So?

ROBERT: How I feel? Disgust, pity, revulsion.

MIRIAM: Pity? You pity him?

ROBERT: He's a tiny, frail old man . . .

MIRIAM: Don't be taken in.

ROBERT: Who says he's ill.

MIRIAM: And you *believe* him?

ROBERT: I don't want to.

MIRIAM: But you do.

ROBERT: We can always get the doctors to look at him. *Our* doctors.

MIRIAM: Then I know who it is.

ROBERT: You do?

MIRIAM: Yes.

ROBERT: How?

MIRIAM: You said *our* doctors. That gave the game away.

ROBERT: You *really* know?

MIRIAM: I do now.

ROBERT: Well, I'd appreciate it if you kept it quiet. Keep it to yourself.

MIRIAM: Well, what do you think I'm likely to do, you idiot? I'm hardly
            likely to shout it from the rooftops. Does Anna know?

ROBERT: Yes.

MIRIAM: And?

ROBERT: No reaction. Said something about building up my kudos.

MIRIAM: Kudos?

ROBERT: Said it would enhance my reputation even though we're clearly
            going to lose.

MIRIAM: You said *we*.

ROBERT: Did I? Slip of the tongue.

MIRIAM: Come here. *(She kisses him)*

ROBERT: What's that for?

MIRIAM: You need to take your mind off work.

ROBERT: I'm not complaining. *(They kiss)*

MIRIAM: Has Anna said anything to you?

ROBERT: *(Anxiously)* No. Said what?

MIRIAM: She said something to me the other day.

ROBERT: Oh?

MIRIAM: Said she thought you were different somehow.

ROBERT: Different?

MIRIAM: Subtle changes. Said she wondered if you were seeing someone.

ROBERT: *(Looks at her)*

MIRIAM: Thought she could smell someone. Someone else. Those were her exact words.

SCENE 9

(The prison. E's cell)

ROBERT: Good morning.

E: Good morning to you.

ROBERT: You seem cheerful.

E: I've been up early.

ROBERT: That makes you cheerful, does it?

E: It makes the day more purposeful.

ROBERT: Oh yes, all those meetings you have to go to. Decisions to take. Run the country.

E: I appreciate the humour. Especially from one so literal. No, it's quite nice early in the morning when there's not a sound. But decisions, yes.

ROBERT: What decisions?

E: They came to see me after you left.

ROBERT: They?

E: The usual characters. I'm sure you know who I mean.

ROBERT: I can guess, yes.

E: So I've been looking at the map.

ROBERT: (Smugly) One country now. The wall's gone.

E: You might well think so. Anyway, I'd appreciate it if you adopted a less frivolous tone.

ROBERT: (Ironically) I'm heartily sorry. So?

E: They asked me to look around.

ROBERT: Look around? What were they? A bunch of estate agents?

E: Not exactly. (Pause) For a host country.

ROBERT: A host country?

E: Yes.

ROBERT: You mean to say . . . ?

E: Yes, well they'll carry on with this pantomime for a little while.

ROBERT: I don't believe it.

E: You didn't really think? (Looks at him) Maybe you did. Anyway, I'm quite looking forward to it. There are one or two speeches I'll be able to make.

ROBERT: The dying embers of resistance.

E: You can laugh, young man. But when you see everything you've dreamed of, worked for . . . toppled, destroyed and callously overthrown, then the caged bird has to sing. (Pause) It's the people I feel sorry for.

ROBERT: You can spare me the social conscience. The people? Why should you care about them?

E: Because they're the ones who will suffer in this unholy marriage, this shotgun wedding. And with your customary arrogance, not to mention smugness, they'll be treated as second class citizens. It's nothing more than a takeover bid. The vultures are already lining up. An ego-boost to that pompous, pontificating cabbage. Ha! A country ruled by a vegetable! Says it all, really. And I can see it clearly now. When I crossed the border in a trip of friendship, a magnanimous gesture, he was already plotting to overthrow me.

ROBERT: And so he has.

E: With the help of his imperialist hooligans.

ROBERT: (Laughs)

E: Why are you laughing?

ROBERT: Trip of friendship, my arse!

E: No, worse still, I was betrayed.

ROBERT: Betrayed?

E: Yes.

ROBERT: By whom?

E: By the younger ones amongst our Allies. If they had only lifted a finger.

ROBERT: But they didn't. They obviously saw you were history. After all, there's no mileage in clapped-out dinosaurs. And didn't it even occur to you, when you journeyed over to the West—in your trip of friendship—that you were doing something your people couldn't. I mean what kind of example was that to set? You unwittingly set a precedent.

E: Maybe it was all part of the trap. Yes, perhaps. But you know, inwardly I rejoiced at seeing parts of the old country. The countryside.

ROBERT: You cried.

E: I did? Oh yes, I did. You read about that? I asked them not to print that. Not to show it. But I couldn't help myself. I went to see my sister, you know.

ROBERT: Your sister?

E: She lived over there.

ROBERT: Over there? That's what we called your part.

E: Great minds, you see.

ROBERT: And what did she have to say to you?

E: She said, Erich, you've put a fucking big wall across our garden.

ROBERT: Did she really? Did she really say that?

E: (Laughs) No, she didn't say that, but her eyes did. Her expression.

ROBERT: Then there was your other mistake.

E: Mistake? You seem very keen to point out my failings today.

ROBERT: Why not? I might as well get my money's worth. After all, we may not be having many more of these conversations.

E: Wouldn't that be a shame? Well then, what mistake?

ROBERT: The one with the trains.

E: I don't see how.

ROBERT: You should have let the holiday makers go. Written them off as a bad loss.

E: Holiday makers? They were hooligans!

ROBERT: If you don't mind me saying, that word is a little old hat. Still, when you're living thirty years or so behind the times.

E: Listen to yourself! Such arrogance!

ROBERT: But you made them get back on the trains, didn't you? Why didn't you just give them a shove with an exit visa and say no more? Then you could seal your borders. But no, your pride meant they had to travel back *through* the sovereign state. And unwittingly, you were endorsing it.

E: In no way . . .

ROBERT: And so they began to stone the railway stations. Just before your celebrations. That must have left you with egg on your faces.

E: The work of agitators. Disparate elements. No, we were let down by our Allies. Especially the ones who counted.

ROBERT: They were humouring you and you failed to see the signs. They put on their best smiles for your birthday celebrations and then they dropped you like an old dishcloth.

E: Maybe . . . maybe you're right. Perhaps I did hold on too long. And maybe I should have handed over to a younger pair of hands. The problem is . . .

ROBERT: Power is addictive.

E: It clouds your judgment.

ROBERT: So does vanity.

E: Are you saying I'm vain?

ROBERT: All those pictures of you. I read some of those old newspapers when I could shake off the tedium. Forty in one magazine!

E: Really? Are you sure? It can't have been. Ah yes, maybe forty as in birthday celebrations for our innovative, founding state.

ROBERT: Floundering state, more like.

E: Yes, yes, very good. I can't help it if I'm photogenic. I mean, whom would you rather have in your papers? Me or that overweight cabbage of yours?

ROBERT: Frankly neither.

E: (Laughs)

ROBERT: Tell me about the map, then.

E: Ah yes, we studied it quite carefully.

ROBERT: And?

E: It would seem I'm persona non grata now in the East. I go against the spirit of reform and change.

ROBERT: What about China?

E: It's a little too far, don't you think? Besides, I could never get on with noodles.

ROBERT: You have my sympathy. So what have you come up with?

E: We thought of South America.

ROBERT: And that's not far?

E: It seemed to suit all purposes. I can learn some Spanish.

ROBERT: South America was a popular destination. After the war, I mean.

E: And there the comparison ends, I hope. I did think about Argentina.

ROBERT: You could travel south and see the penguins.

E: I think I'll have little appetite for travelling . . . once I'm there.

ROBERT: You never know.

E: And I've made one other decision.

ROBERT: Yes?

E: I don't think I need you to represent me after all. You tend to twist my words . . . No, I can manage myself.

ROBERT: But it's your right!

E: Of course. I realise that and it's way too generous. No, I thought if I can rid the state of its legal parasites, you can put the money towards something really worthwhile. Save your money, sonny. And putting up with you and all those little barbs made me realise I'm more than capable of speaking up for myself. And speak up I will.

ROBERT: I suppose you've had plenty of practice over the years.

E: Precisely. I'm glad you see it my way, then.

ROBERT: So it's goodbye, then.

E: Yes it is. I'm sure you're not sorry.

ROBERT: I can't say I am.

E: And look on the bright side.

ROBERT: What's that?

E: You'll have more time for your domestic duties.

ROBERT: What do you mean?

E: Oh, I think you know. (He stares at Robert for a few moments) Must be hard fitting everything in. Work, pleasure, friends, more friends. Does she know, by the way?

ROBERT: (Astonished) What! What are you saying?

E: Nothing. It's just I always recognise a two-timer when I see one.

SCENE 10

(The Library)

ADAM: *(Sleeping)*

LIBRARIAN*:*   *(Walks up to him. Tries to wake him)*

ADAM: *(Groans. Gradually stirs)* Oh, what is it? Where am I?

LIBRARIAN: In the library.

ADAM: Just give me a moment, will you? I've been having the weirdest dreams.

LIBRARIAN: So we noticed. You nearly fell off your chair.

ADAM: What happened to the security guards?

LIBRARIAN: Security guards? What security guards?

ADAM: The ones that threw me out last time.

LIBRARIAN: You must be mistaken. Why would we have security guards? This is a library not a school.

ADAM: No, I suppose not. *(Yawns)* And what happened to the trial? He said he was going to Argentina.

LIBRARIAN: You're not making any sense to me. Anyway, I'm going to have to ask you to leave.

ADAM: So *you're* the security guard?

LIBRARIAN: No.

ADAM: So why should I leave?

LIBRARIAN: Because sleeping is not permitted in the library.

ADAM: But it was *before*.

LIBRARIAN: It isn't now. Not under the new rules.

ADAM: Oh, I see. The *new* rules.

LIBRARIAN: Would you like to see them? I can give you a copy. The Reader's Charter is . . .

ADAM: Oh well, if I have to go, I will. I promise I won't fall asleep when I come in tomorrow. It's these chairs. They're so comfortable.

LIBRARIAN: There is no tomorrow, I'm afraid.

ADAM: Pardon? Isn't that a little gloomy?

LIBRARIAN: No. The library won't be open tomorrow.

ADAM: Oh, so it's a holiday? Well, the day after, then.

LIBRARIAN: That won't be possible either. I'm afraid the library is closing permanently. It's the last day today.

ADAM: The last day? Why? Why's that? Why is it closing?

LIBRARIAN: Extraneous to requirements. There's the newer one across the way. Not more than a stone's throw away.

ADAM: Where's that, then?

LIBRARIAN: It's not quite finished, but you'll soon know when it is.

ADAM: What will happen to *you?*

LIBRARIAN: I don't know. It'll be harder for the rest of the staff.

ADAM: But not for you?

LIBRARIAN: I was thinking of retiring anyway. There's no place for me in the new library.

ADAM: How can you *know* that?

LIBRARIAN: Oh, I just know. Trust me.

ADAM: Do you still want me to leave?

LIBRARIAN: Rules are rules, I'm afraid.

ADAM: Okay, okay. There's just one thing I wanted to ask you before I do.

LIBRARIAN: If I can help, I will.

ADAM: I was hoping to find the way. To Mr. K's house.

(Blackout)

THE GARDENER

CAST LIST

Sarah—Jack's Mother

Jane—Friend of Sarah

Jack—Sarah's Son

Liam—A Gardener

Emma—Friend of Jack

Mrs. Glass—Pub Landlady

SCENE 1

(Sarah's house. Sarah goes to the phone. She picks it up then puts it down. Walks round a few paces, then picks it up again)

SARAH: Hello? Jane? It's Sarah. Look, I'm sorry about the late hour but could you come round? . . . Yes . . . Okay. Fine. See you in half an hour.

(Sits down. Walks round agitatedly. Lights fade for a moment. Doorbell rings. She goes to answer it. Jane enters)

SARAH: Hi.

JANE: Hi, Sarah.

(They enter the sitting room. Pause)

SARAH: Like a coffee?

JANE: Not really. Not at this hour. I'll be awake all night but don't let me stop *you* having one.

(Sarah shakes her head)

JANE: So what's up? I'm sure you haven't asked me round at ten o'clock at night for a coffee?

SARAH: No. *(Pause)* It's Leo. He's not coming back.

JANE: What!

SARAH: I've just had a text from him . . . well, sometime today . . . and it appears I've been unceremoniously dumped.

JANE: You're joking!

SARAH: No, I checked the message. It's genuine all right.

JANE: What did it say . . . if you don't mind me . . . ?

SARAH: It said. Not coming back. Have a good life!

JANE: That bastard! I never liked Leo ever since that time he threw me in the hedge.

SARAH: What a way to do it! No argument. No speeches. No phone call. Two sentences. That's all I'm worth. It seems so spineless. So cowardly.

JANE: That's Leo for you. *(Pause)* I'm sorry. I'm just biased.

SARAH: No, you're right. He's got the backbone of a caterpillar.

JANE: What are you going to tell Jack?

SARAH: For the moment . . . nothing. I'm just going to see if I can make contact. See what this is all about.

JANE: How can someone do something like that? It's so cold. So callous.

SARAH: I think it suits Leo's style. Face to face contact is not his speciality. Send a text or an e-mail instead. Anything to avoid . . .

JANE: But what about Jack? How's he going to.?

SARAH: I really don't know. Leo was always a little indifferent to him. When Jack failed to take up the same interests, he left him to his own devices. *(Pause)* There is another side to this too. I've never been sure that Jack was Leo's.

JANE: What!

SARAH: It was when I went to a conference in the South of France. I met someone I used to know and . . . .

JANE: Did Leo ever suspect.?

SARAH: No, not really. But he did ask more questions about my trip than usual. Perhaps he was missing me then. And if I look at Jack I can see Michael sometimes.

JANE: Michael . . . ? So what happens now? I mean how are *you* feeling?

SARAH: Stunned. Angry. Relieved.

JANE: Relieved?

SARAH: I think a part of me didn't want to go on with it. Slogging it out. *(Pause)* Sometimes it felt that I was living with a stranger in the house. He could be very moody and uncommunicative at times.

JANE: You don't need to remind *me*. And angry?

SARAH: Angry because I didn't get to do it first. And stunned, I suppose, because of the way it happened.

JANE: Do you think there's someone else?

SARAH: Possibly, though he's hardly for all markets. He did start getting phone calls at funny times. As if someone ringing from abroad wasn't quite sure of what time it was here. But then again there are so many of his work colleagues who work all hours.

Fail to see the light of day let alone the colours of their own living-room. So who knows?

JANE: Well, Jack *doesn't*. And you're going to have to tell him. Sometime. Aren't you?

SARAH: Yes, yes. I know.

SCENE 2

(Sarah's house. The doorbell rings)

SARAH: Jack! Get that, will you?

JACK: Why can't *you?*

SARAH: Because I'm drying my hair.

JACK: Okay. *(Jane enters)*

JANE: Hi, Jack. How are you?

JACK: Okay. Yeah. She'll be down in a minute.

JANE: You've let your hair grow long. It suits you.

JACK: Just too lazy to get it cut. Normally Emma cuts it for me.

JANE: Emma?

JACK: Yeah. Friend of mine. Works in the library. Cuts my hair for me and I buy her a pint after.

JANE: I didn't know you were going to pubs.

JACK: *(Puts his fingers to his lips)* Sarah doesn't know.

JANE: How do you get served?

JACK: Em buys the drinks. I give her the dosh. One day I forgot, though, and Mrs. Glass served me anyway. I know they need the money, especially after the Horse and Groom closed.

JANE: A lot of pubs are disappearing. Shops too. That's out of town supermarkets for you.

JACK:	Funny name for a pub landlady, Mrs. Glass. It's like Happy Families. Mrs. Bun, the Baker's wife. But yeah, I hate those out of town places too. You waste all that money in petrol when it could be on your own doorstep. If the pub closes here, there'll be nothing in the village. Just the phone box.

(Enter Sarah)

SARAH:	Hi, Jane.
JANE:	Hi.
JACK:	Right, I'm off then. See you Jane.
JANE:	Yes, see you. *(They sit down)*
SARAH:	Would you like a drink?
JANE:	No, I'm fine. I just popped out for some fresh air and to see how you are.
SARAH:	I'm all right.
JANE:	No news?
SARAH:	Nothing. I can't reach him. The link's well and truly severed. I expect I'll only hear from him when he wants something.
JANE:	And Jack?
SARAH:	I haven't told him yet? *(Jane looks at Sarah)* Yes, yes. I know. I'm just putting it off. I know.
JANE:	What have you said?
SARAH:	That the contract's taking longer than expected. Back at the end of the month.
JANE:	That's ten days.
SARAH:	As if I need reminding. Anyway, how's your work getting on?

JANE: It's okay. I thought I might take a few days off next week.

SARAH: Perhaps we could take a trip out somewhere.

JANE: Maybe. But what about Jack?

SARAH: Oh yes, of course. Well, we can work something out, I'm sure.

JANE: You know if Leo isn't coming back you're going to have to re-think a few things. *(Gets up. Looks out of the window)* The leaves are nearly off the trees now. It's a late autumn.

SARAH: I know. There's a great big swathe of them across the lawn.

JANE: It's a lovely time of year this. I like the dark evenings.

SARAH: That's a point.

JANE: What is?

SARAH: Well, if he's not coming back I'm going to have to get some help in the garden. Get it ready for the winter.

JANE: I wish I had your garden. It's a good size, not like these squitty patches you see with the new homes.

SARAH: Leo used to do quite a bit when he was working from home.

JANE: There *is* someone you could try in the village. At least, I think he's local. There's an ad I've seen in one of the paper shops in town.

SARAH: I might have a look next time I'm in. Anyway, what did you come round for?

JANE: Whatever it was it's gone out of my head.

SCENE 3

(Sarah's house)

SARAH: Please come in.

LIAM: Thanks.

SARAH: I'm sorry I've forgotten your name.

LIAM: Liam.

SARAH: I'd somehow pictured someone older. That's my stereotype that all gardeners are old.

LIAM: Just finished horticultural college. Looking for a job up north.

SARAH: So you won't be around for long?

LIAM: I don't know. Depends what turns up. Not for a while yet, anyway.

(Goes to window) So what is it you want doing?

SARAH: Everything, I suppose. The lawn, some pruning maybe. I leave it to you. If you've been to college you probably know what you're talking about.

LIAM: Try telling that to some of them in the village. I do two gardens a week at present. Oh no, says Mrs. Enderby, don't cut anything back. We always does that in the spring.

SARAH: I promise I won't interfere. Besides, I know very little. You'll have practically a free hand. So when can you come?

LIAM: Depends how often you need me. I've got Wednesdays and Fridays free.

SARAH: That would be fine. Twice a week, then. There's a bit of a backlog as you'll see. Leo didn't get out much lately.

LIAM: Leo?

SARAH: Yes, he's still in South Africa. He'll be away for a while.

LIAM: See you Wednesday then.

(Liam leaves. Sarah goes to the phone and picks it up)

SARAH: Jane, I'm going to tell Jack this evening . . . I thought that would please you.

So you don't need to nag me about it any more. He's going to ask questions when the gardener turns up, so I thought I'd pre-empt it . . . Yes. Twice a week . . . You don't think that's too much? Only I forgot to say how many hours. Yes. See you soon.

SCENE 4

(Jack's bedroom)

JACK: She's behaving quite oddly at the moment.

EMMA: How do you mean?

JACK: Kind of quiet, preoccupied.

EMMA: Perhaps she's busy with stuff.

JACK: And the other thing. She was showing some bloke round. They were walking round the garden.

EMMA: You don't think she's selling the house?

JACK: Bloody hope not! I'm fed up with moving places. Just as soon as you get settled, get to know people, you're up and away again. It was mainly because of Leo.

EMMA: The old man?

JACK: Yeah. Work moved him around like some kind of yoyo. He's in South Africa at the moment. I think she's missing him. First of all, she was all jolly when he went away. You know, doing things. Going out more. But now she's moping round the house most of the time.

EMMA: Do you think it's having to move that's done it?

JACK: Yeah, could be. I think she likes it here.

EMMA: Do *you*?

JACK: Yeah, it's not bad. Bit snotty-nosed in the village sometimes. You know, these commuter types. I think they think I'm a bit of an oik.

EMMA: And *are* you?

JACK: Dunno. Perhaps all long hair means oiks to them. I've seen the dirty looks we get when we're in the beer garden.

EMMA: Well, you're with *me*, aren't you? And *I'm* over eighteen. I'm legal.

JACK: Perhaps they think I'm your toy-boy.

EMMA: Well, hardly. But it would be a shame if you had to move.

JACK: Maybe I could stay. I wouldn't have to go with them. Get a job. I'll be sixteen in a few months.

EMMA: Jobs round here? What *planet* are you on?

JACK: You know what pisses me off the most about them, is they never ask you about these things. Never say, Jack, how would you feel about a change of scene? They just assume I'll get up and go and go trotting after them. Well not this time! I'm fed up with moving. I've got friends here.

EMMA: Friends, Jack? You're using the plural. There's me, so who are the others?

JACK: *(Goes towards her as if to hit her playfully)* I'll have to think about that. I'll have to advertise, won't I?

EMMA: 'Friends wanted for thoughtful, studious, intellectual type. Likes . . .

JACK: Leave it out!

EMMA: I think you're only friends with me because I can cut hair. I know.

JACK: Bollocks, Em! You're just you. That's what I like about you. You're not somebody *else* like some of those snotpiles in the village.

EMMA: All right! Shall we go down the pub and have a drink?

JACK: What are we celebrating?

EMMA: Me not being a snotpile and some momentous changes coming into your life.

JACK: Don't say that, Emma. I tell you, there's *no* way I'm moving and going with them this time.

EMMA: Bravely spoken. Let's go!

SCENE 5

(Sarah's house)

JANE: So how did it go with Jack?

SARAH: You want the official version or the unofficial version?

JANE: I'm happy to hear both.

SARAH: Well, *he* brought about the conversation. I was trying to put it off . . .

JANE: What did he say?

SARAH: First of all, he says, I'm not fucking moving. Just out of the blue. He was really off. And I said, moving? What gave you that idea? And he said, you showing people round the house and that. Where did you get that from, I said. That's just Liam. He's coming to help with the garden. So he asked why and I just sat down and cried. He just stood there and then I had to tell him . . . the *whole thing.*

JANE: How did he react?

SARAH: I'm not sure react is the word. *(Pause)* Very little, anyway. Didn't seem to bother him. Well, he's never been around that much. Jack had got it into his head that we were moving and he was more worried about that. Then he said why do we need someone to do the garden? I said I hadn't time and Jack's never shown the slightest interest.

JANE: Sounds like he's tetchy about another male on his domain. *His* territory. Anyway, so it could have been a lot worse?

SARAH: It's funny about the moving. Maybe he's got an attachment here.

JANE: Emma?

SARAH: Or possibly someone at the college.

JANE: You don't think it's a delayed reaction to Leo. That he's holding it all back . . . till the news finally sinks in.

SARAH: Who knows? It could be his way of dealing with it. But I don't know. He and Leo have never been that fond of each other. Jack's always been quite self-sufficient. *Only* children sometimes are.

JANE: You never thought about . . . ?

SARAH: Never seemed to have the time. It sounds silly but I was always so busy. Then when I did have the time, there was little inclination. Things were becoming more difficult between us and . . .

          (Doorbell rings) That's probably Liam.

JANE: Okay, I'll leave you to it. I'll call by tomorrow. *(Kisses Sarah)* Bye!

SARAH: Bye!

SCENE 6

(Jack's bedroom)

EMMA: So you must be pleased, then?

JACK: Pleased? About what?

EMMA: The fact you're not moving.

JACK: Yeah, yeah.

EMMA: So he was just the gardener?

JACK: Yeah. Looks like it. Apparently the old man's not coming back. Done a runner.

EMMA: What a shit! And she *never* knew?

JACK: No. Sent her a text. Got no bottle.

EMMA: What a way to do it! I'd have knocked his teeth out!

JACK: You probably could and all! *(Pause)*

EMMA: Have you always called them Leo and Sarah?

JACK: Yeah. Ever since I can remember. They encouraged me to do it.

EMMA: I suppose it was trendy at the time.

JACK: Either that or they didn't want to own up to their parental role. *(Pause)*

EMMA: Did you ever wish you'd had brothers and sisters?

JACK: No, not really. Never given it much thought. A brother, maybe, but not a sister.

EMMA: You've got me, anyway. *(Laughs)* Big sister takes little brother to the pub.

JACK: Piss off!

EMMA: That's no way to talk to family. They probably think we're an item. A couple. By the way, that new lad, the gardener. Do you like him?

JACK: I've hardly spoken to him.

EMMA: He looks well fit.

JACK: Trust you! *(Pause)* When did you see him?

EMMA: I came round, but you weren't back from college. He was doing the apple trees. Nice bum. I was holding the ladder for him.

JACK: Well, so long as that was all you were holding.

EMMA: *(Clouts him)* Said they should have been done *ages* ago.

JACK: I reckon Leo knew bugger all. He thought he did but he was useless. *I* could have told him that. It's a basic principle of gardening.

EMMA: Ooh! Hark at you! Anyway, I said to him we'd go for a drink one evening.

JACK: We? You mean *you two?* Hasn't he got a girlfriend?

EMMA: I meant us three. Can't have my baby brother chewing his fists with jealousy.

JACK: No, you go. I'll be all right.

EMMA: You stick in the mud! What's wrong? We can *all* go.

JACK:	Yeah, but I'd need to know him a bit better first. Especially if it's someone working for you.
EMMA:	For *Sarah*, not you. And anyway, if you don't go you won't get to know him.
JACK:	I'll think about it.
EMMA:	You're *put out*, aren't you?
JACK:	Put out? *Me?*
EMMA:	Yes, *you.* That I asked him.
JACK:	No.
EMMA:	Yes, you are, Jack Medlock. I know you well enough. These are changes threatening your cosy little world. I bet you're the kind who likes to keep his friends in little boxes. Tidy compartments. Some people are like that. Perhaps scared that their friends will all run off with each other.
JACK:	Bollocks, Em! Anyway, what about my hair? It's getting a bit long. What do you think?
EMMA:	I think it's a good change of subject. And no, it's quite sexy. I'll have to look at my busy schedule. See if I can fit you in.

SCENE 7

(Sarah's garden. Liam is working there. Jack walks by)

LIAM: All right?

JACK: *(Guardedly)* Yeah. Fine. *(Pause)* It's a bit chilly, innit?

LIAM: It's not too bad. I tell myself I'm lucky to be working in the winter. One of the hazards of gardening. Everything tends to shut down.

JACK: Suppose so. (Pause) Sarah says you're going up north maybe.

LIAM: Sarah? Oh yes. Depends. One of those National Trust places. Some big project with the gardens. Haven't heard anything yet.

JACK: Have you always done this kind of work?

LIAM: Yeah, I have. It's all I know.

JACK: You never fancied going for the big money?

LIAM: What? Working in town? In an office or something? You must be joking!

JACK: Doesn't seem too bad to me.

LIAM: Nine to five office stuff. *(Shudders)* I couldn't bear to be inside, cooped up, chained to a desk . . .

JACK: No, it's better outside freezing your bollocks off.

LIAM: Funnily enough, that's one thing I've never had.

JACK: What? What's that?

LIAM: Frozen bollocks. *(Jack laughs)* What about you? What kind of things do you want to do?

JACK: Dunno. Carry on at college. Uni, maybe. Delay the inevitable.

LIAM: There's a friend of mine, in Germany, right. Finished studying at 35! Amazing, isn't it?

JACK: Is he a slow learner?

LIAM: *(Laughs)* I'll have to tell him you said that.

JACK: Not bad, is it? Few years work, then he can retire.

LIAM: Not bad at all. Oh yeah, *(hitches up his trousers)* your friend Emma said about going out for a drink one evening. You coming? She said about the three of us going.

JACK: Dunno. Got a shitload of coursework to do.

LIAM: I'm sure you could sneak away from it. You *do* go to the pub, though?

JACK: Yeah. Emma usually goes up and buys the drinks in case there's any problem.

LIAM: Never is. Mrs. Glass always used to serve me but Rob the barman usually gave one of his long, searching looks. A nod from Mrs. G does the trick. Anyway, you should *come,* you old stick in the mud. Emma's good fun. I like her.

JACK: Yeah. Probably. I'll see.

SCENE 8

(Sarah's house)

JANE: So how's it working out?

SARAH: Better. Better than I expected. And I've heard from Leo.

JANE: More than two sentences, I hope.

SARAH: Yes. Apparently, I can buy him out. His share of the house, that is.

JANE: And what about payments? For you and Jack?

SARAH: He was a bit evasive about that.

JANE: I'm not surprised.

SARAH: Seeing as it's going to be so difficult to get hold of him, perhaps I should settle for a lower price on the house.

JANE: But he's supposed to . . .

SARAH: If I don't know where he is . . . which country, it's going to be a fat lot of use. Perhaps I should just cut my losses.

JANE: What else did he say?

SARAH: Not a lot.

JANE: Did he ask about Jack?

SARAH: No, but you wouldn't expect him to, would you?

JANE: And Jack?

SARAH: Doesn't seem to mind a bit. As I said, he and Leo didn't have much time for each other. All in all, things seem to be okay at the moment.

JANE: That gardener of yours is a bit of a find.

SARAH: Dedicated, I think the word is. Takes it all quite seriously. Knows his stuff.

JANE: Quite handsome too.

SARAH: I hadn't noticed.

JANE: Really?

SARAH: I've been too busy. I hardly see him, except when he comes for his money.

JANE: It's looking good. If I had a decent garden, I'd have him. Or perhaps I'd have him anyway.

SARAH: Re-run the Lady Chatterley story.

JANE: I've never read it. But I think perhaps I should.

SARAH: Listen to you. He's a *boy*, for heaven's sake!

JANE: He must be what . . . twenty two? Jack's a boy, but he's growing fast too. Perhaps you hadn't noticed that either. *(Pause)* Well, I should get back. Don't want to keep you from your duties. Call me.

SARAH: I will.

(Looks out into garden. Motions to Liam "cup of tea?")

SCENE 9

(The pub)

JACK: So is Liam coming?

EMMA: I left a message on his machine. I think he drinks here anyway.

MRS. GLASS: What can I get you?

EMMA: Two pints of bitter, Mrs. G.

MRS. GLASS: When I was younger women never drank pints.

EMMA: This one does. And anyway, halves go down quicker.

MRS. GLASS: I don't mind if they do. Trade's been bad this month. I keep having to send the bitter back. That last brewery was rubbish on ullage.

JACK: What's that?

MRS. GLASS: The beer what don't get drunk.

EMMA: Good pint, though. Nice dark beer for the winter.

MRS. GLASS: Hark at you. You'll be writing those beer guides next.

EMMA: Wouldn't mind if I did. Travelling round the country sampling all the different ones.

JACK: You'd get as fat as a pig.

MRS. GLASS: *(Passes beer over)* There you are. And Emma . . .

EMMA: Yes?

MRS. GLASS: Better if Jack doesn't come to the bar when we've got strangers here.

(Motions to far corner)

EMMA: Sorry, yes. I usually buy them anyway. *(They take the beer and sit down)*

JACK: What was that?

EMMA: I have to keep little brother out of the way.

JACK: Less of the *little*.

EMMA: *(Pause)* How's your work going?

JACK: Got an essay for Monday.

EMMA: Ah, the joys of studying. You know what Bethany said when she started working? She said she couldn't get used to coming home in the evening and *no* homework.

(Sarah enters pub)

JACK: Paradise! *(Sips beer)* Shit!

EMMA: What's up? What is it?

JACK: It's Sarah, that's what!

EMMA: What's *she* doing here? She *never* comes down here.

JACK: Dunno. Maybe meeting that old goss across the way.

EMMA: Jane?

JACK: I've got to get out of here. She'll do her nut if she sees me!

(Leaves quickly. For a few moments, Emma sits on her own.
Sarah looks over. Sees Emma)

SARAH: Hello, Emma.

EMMA: Hello, Mrs. Medlock. Don't usually see you here.

SARAH: No, well, I fancied a change. A different atmosphere from my sitting room. I finished my deadlines, so here I am.

EMMA: Must be nice working from home. That's what Jane does, isn't it? I've always fancied it myself.

SARAH: Has its drawbacks, though. It can be lonely at times, working on your own. Sometimes you don't get out, see people. I often wish I had a small office somewhere.

EMMA: Oh yeah. Where would you have it?

SARAH: In town, maybe. But it's an extra expense and it's certainly not practical at the moment.

EMMA: *(Pause)* Er, Jack told me about Leo. I'm sorry.

SARAH: *(Slightly surprised)* Oh yes? Well, you needn't be. *I'm* not.

(Looks at Emma's empty glass) Would you like another one, Emma?

EMMA: No, I'm fine thanks. I ought to be getting back. See you.

SARAH: Yes. Bye Emma. *(Emma leaves. Sarah is alone at the bar)*

MRS. GLASS: What would you like?

SARAH: Campari and soda, please.

MRS. GLASS: I'll just have to go to the cellar and get another bottle. Won't be a minute.

(Silence. Liam enters. He looks around then comes up to Sarah)

LIAM: Hello, Mrs. Medlock.

SARAH: Oh, hello, Liam.

LIAM: Don't often see you here.

SARAH: This is becoming a catchphrase round here.

LIAM: *(Puzzled)* Pardon?

SARAH: That's what Emma said.

LIAM: Emma? Is *she* here?

SARAH: No, I'm afraid you just missed her. I'm surprised you didn't pass her on the way.

LIAM: I came across the fields. There's a footpath.

(Mrs. Glass passes drink)

SARAH*:*   *(To Liam)* And what will you have?

LIAM: Pint of mild, please.

MRS. GLASS: No mild till Monday.

LIAM: Bitter, then, please.

(Silence. Mrs. Glass hands over bitter.)

MRS. GLASS: Three eighty.

SARAH: Thanks. And have one yourself, Mrs. Glass.

MRS. GLASS: That's nice of you, Mrs. Bedlock. Babycham? *(Pause)* Five fifty, please. *(Pause)*

SARAH: *(To Liam)* She always calls me Mrs. Bedlock. I never know if she's being funny or if she really thinks that is my name.

LIAM: Always been a bit deaf, has Hilda. One night she didn't hear Rob call last orders and went on serving till half past.

SARAH: I think I'd come more often if the pub stayed open later.

LIAM: Would you?

SARAH: I sometimes look at the clock around ten and think I'd go down for a drink if I knew it would be open late.

LIAM: Ah, now you would have liked the Horse and Groom. Always having lock-ins Geoff was. Used to ask you ever so politely, would you mind drawing the curtains, please? And so you would and he'd carry on serving.

SARAH: I don't remember seeing the Horse and . . .

LIAM: Tucked away off Back Lane. All the ex-coppers used to drink there. I suppose that's why you were able to carry on drinking.

SARAH: Maybe we could go there after.

LIAM: If only! The brewery closed it, didn't they? It's turned into tea rooms. *(Takes a long swig of beer)* I wonder why Emma went home. Did she say she was coming back?

SARAH: No, nothing.

LIAM: That's funny. The three of us were meeting for a drink.

SARAH: *Three?* Who's the other person?

LIAM: *(Anxiously)* Er. John. You don't know him. It's a bit of a trek so he may not . . . .

SARAH: *Jack* doesn't come to the pub, Liam?

LIAM: Jack? No. I've never seen him here. Why?

SARAH: I wouldn't want him to be drinking under age.

LIAM: No, no. *(He finishes his beer)*

SARAH: By the way, the garden's looking really great now.

LIAM: Thanks.

SARAH: *(Noticing his empty glass)* Same again, Liam?

LIAM: Thanks, but I should get this.

SARAH: Put your money away! We're celebrating an auspicious occasion.

LIAM: Oh yeah? What's that, then?

SARAH: Me being in the pub, though regrettably not the Horse and Groom, and the completion of deadlines *(To Mrs. Glass)* Same again, please.

SCENE 10

(Jack is in the sitting room. Knock on door)

JACK: Who is it?

EMMA: It's me, Emma.

JACK: *(Opens door)* I thought you were in the pub?

EMMA: Change of plan.

JACK: I thought you were meeting Liam?

EMMA: Just felt a bit awkward with Sarah there. Not being funny . . .

JACK: Sarah? No, no. That's the last thing you want. Parents.

EMMA: You said *parents* . . .

JACK: You know what I mean. *(Pause)* Anyway, that bastard Leo's not coming back.

EMMA: That's a bit harsh.

JACK: Is it? You don't know the *half* of things, Em.

EMMA: Meaning what?

JACK: I don't want to talk about it.

EMMA: Talk about what?

JACK: *(Angrily) Just* leave it!

EMMA: It's not like you . . .

JACK: Leo was no saint, believe me.

EMMA: How do you know?

JACK:	*(Points to his eyes)* Eyes. Places. People. People other than Sarah. Meeting people in odd places.
EMMA:	I see. So he had somebody else?
JACK:	I said people, Em. That's in the plural, in case you hadn't noticed.
EMMA:	So how did you find out?
JACK:	At the railway station one evening. Meeting someone. They were saying goodbye. I ducked behind the coffee kiosk.
EMMA:	It could have just been a friend.
JACK:	Not the way those goodbyes were going. It was the marathon tongue sandwich.
EMMA:	Jack!
JACK:	I started watching him after that. When he had calls, I lifted up the phone to listen. All female. Different voices. Different lies, different confessions. I would listen to him on the phone and I thought how easy it was to tell when he was lying. So easy.
EMMA:	Does Sarah know?
JACK:	I don't think so. He was clever at covering his trail. But anyway, by that time everything had blown cold. And now he's staying away. Probably with one of his telephone floosies. I used to try and picture what they looked like.
EMMA:	And it doesn't bother you him not coming back?
JACK:	Why should it? He wasn't interested in me and I wasn't interested in him.
EMMA:	But interested enough to find out what he was up to?

JACK: I was curious. I wanted to find out. I thought it might be useful.

EMMA: *Useful?* Useful for what?

JACK: I dunno. I just did. I quite enjoyed playing the private detective at railway stations.

EMMA: And I thought this was a *normal* household!

JACK: Doesn't exist, Em. It's all secrets and lies. And if you want to know something else . . .

EMMA: Yes?

JACK: I don't think I'm his.

EMMA: You *what?*

JACK: You heard. I'm not his.

EMMA: You're just being silly. You're angry and . . .

JACK: No. No, I'm not. I don't *look* like him, don't *feel* . . . .

EMMA: You're bound to . . . .

JACK: Save all that stuff! I know what I *feel.* I *know!*

EMMA: Does Sarah know you think.?

JACK: No. But oddly enough, it was something she said one day that got me thinking. *(Pause)* Anyway, why's she down the pub? She *never* goes out to them.

EMMA: Said she was celebrating. Something about deadlines.

JACK: But she's always finishing those. It's no big deal.

EMMA: Perhaps she thought *we'd* be down there. Maybe she's been doing her own private detective work.

JACK: What! To catch us out, you mean?

EMMA: Maybe. I don't know. Something brought her down there, anyway.

JACK: Something or *someone?*

EMMA: I don't know. Perhaps it's her new lifestyle. Or maybe she's meeting Jane.

JACK: Jane wouldn't go to pubs. They're way beneath her. Not her scene.

EMMA: Anyway, I'd better go.

JACK: You going back?

EMMA: No, she might still be down there.

JACK: She won't bite!

EMMA: You can talk! You ran a mile when you saw her.

JACK: Yes, but I *live* here. You *don't*. I'd never hear the end of it.

EMMA: No, I'll leave it. I'll tell Liam I'm sorry. Arrange something for another night. See ya!

JACK: Yeah. See ya! *(Jack kisses Emma goodnight)*

SCENE 11

(The pub)

SARAH: *(Tipsy)* Have another one, Liam.

LIAM: I'd better be going, Mrs. Medlock.

SARAH: Sarah, please. If we're going to be drinking partners, then drop the Mrs. Medlock bit. *(Motions to Mrs. Glass)*

LIAM: Yeah, okay.

SARAH: Funny name, don't you think?

LIAM: What is?

SARAH: Medlock. Sounds like wedlock, doesn't it? That's another thing I'm not very good at.

LIAM: Sorry? None of this is making any sense, Sarah.

SARAH: Oh, Liam, of course, you don't *know.*

LIAM: Know what?

SARAH: I might as well tell you. He's not coming back?

LIAM: *(Panics)* Jack, you mean?

SARAH: No, no. Leo, of course. It's all over. Decided to stay out there. I'll be changing my name back.

LIAM: I see. Yes, of course.

SARAH: So I'll be plain Roberts again. It's quite safe, isn't it? Not like Medlock. Sounds like hemlock, I sometimes think. That's poison, you know.

LIAM: Yes, I *do* know.

SARAH: Sorry. Of course, you do. That's your trade and very good at it you are too.

(She runs a hand momentarily through his hair).
           What's your family name, by the way?

LIAM: O'Connor.

SARAH: Proper Irish. Sounds good. Quite dignified.

LIAM: I've never been, to my shame.

SARAH: Been? Been where?

LIAM: To Ireland. *(Pause)* Someone told me the Americans had bought up some of the lakes.

SARAH: Lakes? How can you buy up lakes? Going back to their roots probably. They have a thing about that. No, you should go.

LIAM: You're right. I should.

SARAH: Then why don't you?

LIAM: I'm fine here. I'm happy. If I went, I might end up staying.

SARAH: Bad idea, Liam. We need you here. *(She hiccoughs. Falls off chair)* Whoops!

LIAM: You certainly do. Here. *(Offers hand. Half pulls her up)*

SARAH: It's this stupid knee of mine.

LIAM: Must be a chemical reaction to alcohol.

MRS. GLASS: *(Anxiously)* Everything all right?

LIAM: Fine, yeah. *(To Sarah)* I think we should go after this one.

SARAH: But we've only just . . . .

LIAM: I think we'd better. There's always other times.

                         (Sarah looks at Liam for a moment)

SARAH: I've enjoyed this drink, Liam. I can talk to *you*. I can tell you things I can't talk about with Jack around.

LIAM: I know. *(Finishes pint)* Let's be going, eh?

MRS. GLASS: Do you want me to ring for a taxi?

LIAM: No, it's okay.

SARAH: I might need some guiding home, though.

LIAM: Yes, of course. *(He straightens her up)* Hold on to me.

                  (They walk back. Church clock strikes eleven)

SARAH: What time is that?

LIAM: Eleven. Nearly chucking out time, anyway.

SARAH: If only we had the Horse and Groom. Now that's what I call civilized. *(Burps)*

SCENE 12

(Sarah's house, the next morning. Sarah moves slowly round living room, gingerly.
Sits down. Doorbell rings. Sarah answers it)

SARAH: Oh, Jane. It's you.

JANE: Well, there's a welcome*! (Steps in. Looks at Sarah)* You okay?

SARAH: Just had a late night.

JANE: You went out?

SARAH: Yes.

JANE: Anywhere special?

SARAH: Just the pub?

JANE: The *pub?* But you *never* go to the pub! What's the occasion?

SARAH: There was none. I just fancied it.

JANE: You didn't go on your own?

SARAH: No.

JANE: So who did you go with?

SARAH: Village life is really getting to you, I can see. *(She hesitates.)*
           Liam.

JANE: Liam? This is a new development. Did you ask him out?

SARAH: No, of course not. I was down the pub and he happened to
           be there. Says he was waiting for someone but they never
           showed.

JANE: But you *never* go to the pub.

SARAH: I do now.

JANE: So you consoled each other?

SARAH: In a way, yes.

JANE: You look a bit rough.

SARAH: Haven't had a drink in ages. Thought I deserved it.

JANE: You didn't drive?

SARAH: Of course not.

JANE: How did you get back?

SARAH: You're beginning to sound like my mother. He brought me
             back.

JANE: I see.

SARAH: And what does 'I see' mean? You're making it sound like . . .

JANE: You fancy him, don't you?

SARAH: *(Looks away)* Don't be absurd! I'm old enough . . .

JANE: So what? Go for it! Life after Leo. Why not?

SARAH: We *just* had a drink!

JANE: Sounds like more than one.

SARAH: Jane, just piss off, will you?

JANE: Sorry. *(Pause)* Anyway, I'm very pleased for you.

SCENE 13

(Jack's bedroom)

JACK: Did you sort it with Liam?

EMMA: Yeah. I gave him a call.

JACK: And?

EMMA: Said you had to scarper because Sarah came in. I didn't fancy hearing childhood anecdotes or the break-up with Leo, so I legged it too and tried to phone him.

JACK: Yeah.

EMMA: Left his mobile at home, didn't he? Says he hates it going off when he's out.

JACK: Doesn't that defeat the object?

EMMA: Of what?

JACK: Of a mobile. It's a stationary, not a mobile.

EMMA: Yes, very clever. Anyway, he was quite pissed off.

JACK: Pissed off? Why?

EMMA: Had to walk Sarah home. She was *well* gone. I'm surprised you didn't hear anything.

JACK: You know me. Once I hit the pillow. But no, I didn't hear anything.

EMMA: Kept saying we must do it again sometime.

JACK:	Do *what* again?
EMMA:	Go out. I don't think Liam's that keen.
JACK:	But she *can't* do that!
EMMA:	No. It's a bit awkward when you work for someone.
JACK:	That's not what I meant, but yeah there's that too.
EMMA:	What did you mean, Jack?
JACK:	Nothing.
EMMA:	*(Looks at him for a moment)* Sure? Anyway, I thought we could go for a drink later.
JACK:	I've got this essay to finish. It's a real pain in the arse.
EMMA:	I thought you were doing that last night.
JACK:	I was but I didn't feel like it in the end. Watched telly. Bugger all on.
EMMA:	That's telly for you. A whole variety of crap on an unholy variety of channels.
JACK:	If you say so, Em.
EMMA:	I do. Come on, let's take a walk. Let's mobilize that television bottom of yours.

SCENE 14

(Sarah's garden)

JACK: Hiya!

LIAM: Hi! How's it going?

JACK: Yeah, all right. And you?

LIAM: Fine. Just finished sorting out the hedge, now I'll take a look at the pond.

JACK: What's there to look at? Looks all right to me.

LIAM: Clearing out, mainly. It's leaves that are the problem. Makes the water go bad if you don't get them out. What's in the pond, anyway?

JACK: Don't know. No fish, if that's what you mean. Saw a frog once. It was making a noise.

LIAM: Calling, probably. The call of a lonely heart. *(Laughs)* Let's take a look. *(Pause)* I'd love to have a pond this size in my garden.

JACK: Have this one, if you like.

LIAM: No room, mate. Ours is only a tiny postage stamp of a garden. *(Pause)*

JACK: I hear you had to walk Sarah back the other night.

LIAM: Yeah, she was a bit tired.

JACK: Pissed, more like! She always farts when she's pissed.

LIAM: I prefer tired.

JACK: Em reckons she's got a thing for you.

LIAM: Don't talk stupid!

JACK: She might be right. Gross!

LIAM: Who? Her or me?

JACK: Sarah, of course. Come to think of it, I *have* seen her looking out of the window when you're working. *(Grins)* Admiring that arse of yours.

(Liam throws seed-heads at him. Jack laughs.)

LIAM: Not for much longer, anyway.

JACK: What?

LIAM: The trip up north. They want me to start on the gardens in January. There's a massive amount of clearing to do. They're trying to get it ready for the summer.

JACK: So that's it, then? But you'll come back, though? Weekends?

LIAM: It's a bit too far. It'll be working to a tight schedule.

JACK: Now where have I heard that before?

LIAM: Not from me you ain't. Anyway, you can come up and see me. There'll be room to stay.

(Liam pulls up a clump of grass. Examines it)

JACK: What is it?

LIAM: Take a look, mate.

JACK: What is it?

LIAM: Tiny frog. Must be this year's. Should be asleep.

JACK: It's all this mild weather. Confused the poor thing.

LIAM: Aha. So you *do* know something?

JACK: What do you mean something?

LIAM: All this disinterested lark. It's just an act. I mean, you can't live here and not notice things. *(Pause)* So when I'm up north you can start sorting the garden out.

JACK: Carry on the good work, you mean?

LIAM: Yeah. I'll tell you what to do.

JACK: I bet you will.

LIAM: Yeah. I'll write it all down.

JACK: And if I don't?

LIAM: I'll come back and throw you in the pond.

JACK: That means you'll have to ring me to find out how it's going.

LIAM: And see if my instructions are being obeyed? Yeah, I'm sure we can arrange that. Anyway, you can help me get these leaves out for a start.

JACK: There's a fishing net in the shed. Better than using that old rake.

LIAM: Okay. You can show me.

SCENE 15

(Sarah's house)

EMMA: Hi, Mrs. Medlock.

SARAH: Emma.

EMMA: Is Jack in?

SARAH: Don't think he's back from college yet. He's been hard at it all week. Suddenly taken on a new lease of life. Taking it more seriously. You haven't been speaking to him, have you?

EMMA: No.

SARAH: Well someone has and I'm very grateful.

EMMA: We were just going to go for a walk. *(Long pause. Birdsong)*

SARAH: Where do you go for your walks?

EMMA: Nowhere special. Along the river sometimes.

SARAH: That's something *I* should do more. I'm always too busy cooped up inside to notice things.

EMMA: What things?

SARAH: Everything. Things around you. Fields, hedgerows.

EMMA: That's funny. Jack's got more into that too. Never used to pay any attention . . .

SARAH: Well, I'm sure it's down to your good influence, Emma. He listens to *you*.

EMMA: I doubt it.

SARAH: Anyway, I'm going to get out more. You can't judge things from behind the wheel of a car.

EMMA: That's true. That's what Liam says. He hates the things.

SARAH: Like being in a goldfish bowl. Well, I'm determined to break out on my own. I've been stuck in that stupid house for far too long. Cocooned in a stupid marriage that went nowhere. I should have done it earlier. *Much* earlier. *(Pause)* Anyway, here's me rabbiting on. I'll tell Jack you've called. Bye, Emma.

EMMA: Goodbye, Mrs. Medlock. *(To herself)* The new Jack, eh? I wonder what's been going on there.

SCENE 16

(Sarah's house. Sarah is looking out of the window into the garden. She watches Liam cutting back the bushes. He shows Jack how to do it. Ruffles his hair when he finishes)

SCENE 17

(Sarah's house later the same day)

JANE: I enjoyed that book you lent me.

SARAH: Good.

JANE: It was a good read.

SARAH: I'm glad.

JANE: Jack tells me you've joined a gym or something.

SARAH: Hardly. It's just an aerobics class.

JANE: There's a bit of a revolution afoot these days.

SARAH: What do you mean?

JANE: The new Sarah. The fitness Sarah. The back to nature Sarah. And unless I'm very much mistaken I could have sworn I saw you looking at bikes in town.

SARAH: You're not and I was.

JANE: Well, I'm all for it.

SARAH: I'm so glad I've got your approval. It's such a relief.

JANE: You could always borrow mine. I don't use it much.

SARAH: Thanks, but I need to get one of my own anyway.

JANE: We could go out cycling, then. Together. Find some pubs, seeing as you're now into them.

SARAH: I thought it was *you* who didn't like them?

JANE: Me? No. Whatever gave you that idea? *(Pause)* By the way, there's a light on in your shed.

SARAH: There can't be!

JANE: *(Pointing)* See for yourself!

SARAH: *(Looking out)* So there is!

JANE: It can't be Liam, can it?

SARAH: At nine o'clock in the evening? Hardly.

JANE: Unless he's doing some tidying up before he goes. *(Pause) (She gasps)* You don't think it's someone stealing the tools? A few places round here have had stuff nicked recently.

SARAH: You're not serious?

JANE: They sell them off at car-boot sales. It was in the local rag.

SARAH: I think we should take a look.

JANE: Why not call the police?

SARAH: The police? You must be joking! It takes half an hour to get through on the phone. They divert you anywhere and everywhere and then they say they're too busy. A week later, they send a spotty schoolboy round and say there's nothing they can do. No. Let's go out there *together*. See if we can scare them off.

JANE: I don't like this, Sarah. Shouldn't we try . . . ?

SARAH: Come on.

(They approach the shed)

JANE: I can't hear anything.

SARAH: Neither can I.

JANE: If they were taking things, we'd hear them.

SARAH: The light's not moving either. Looks like a paraffin lamp.

(Sarah peers through the window. Stares for a moment, disbelievingly)

JANE: Sarah! What is it? Sarah? *(Muffled sound of Liam moaning)*

SARAH: *(Peers through the window)* It's Liam. I can see him.)

JANE: What's he doing?

SARAH: I should have thought that was obvious. He's with someone.

JANE: What! In *your* shed? Who is it?

SARAH: I can't see. *(Steps back to avoid being seen)* It must be Emma. I've seen them down the pub together.

JANE: What a cheek! In *your* garden! Still, I suppose they can't go to *his* place and maybe not *hers* either. What are you going to do?

SARAH: Enjoy the moment.

JANE: *(Shocked)* Sarah! Come on! Leave it! Talk to him in the morning.

SARAH: He's leaving anyway. At the end of the week. My beautiful gardener!

JANE: *(Pulls Sarah back. Takes a brief look through the gap in the curtains. Gives a gasp of surprise)* Oh! Oh no!

SCENE 18

(Jack's bedroom)

EMMA: Hi, Jack.

JACK: Hi, Em.

EMMA: How's things?

JACK: *(Subdued)* Okay.

EMMA: Haven't seen you for a few days.

JACK: Yeah, I haven't seen you for a few days either.

EMMA: You been busy?

JACK: Yeah. Kind of.

EMMA: *(Pause)* You all right, Jack?

JACK: Yeah, I'm all right, Jack. Why shouldn't I be?

EMMA: Dunno. You seem . . . .

JACK: What?

EMMA: Different. Bit quiet.

JACK: Am I?

EMMA: Yes, you are. Not your usual bubbly self.

JACK: I leave that to you, Em. That's your department.

EMMA: *(Pause)* There's nothing wrong, then?

JACK: No.

EMMA: *(Pause)* You can tell *me,* you know.

JACK: Listen. Everything's fine.

EMMA: Well then, do you fancy going for a drink later?

JACK: Nah. I think I'll give it a miss. I'm a bit knackered. I'll stay in.

EMMA: *(Looks at book on table)* Oh. What are you reading?

JACK: Take a look.

EMMA: *(Reads aloud)* Pond Maintenance Made Easy? Since when have you been interested in ponds?

JACK: Since now.

EMMA: *(Surprised)* It's not like you. It's a bit of a conversion.

JACK: Conversion? What do you mean? Why do you say that?

EMMA: Well, you've never shown the slightest interest.

JACK: It's Liam. He wants me to do one or two things in the garden till we . . .

EMMA: I see.

JACK: Get someone to replace him.

EMMA: Really? I thought from what Sarah said he was unreplaceable.

JACK: Irreplaceable, Em. You should know that.

EMMA: The irritable pedant rises to the bait.

JACK: You what? Oh, I see. Sorry. It's just a late night, Em. I'll be all right.

EMMA: *(Looking at book)* Did he give you this?

JACK: What? No, I got it at college.

EMMA: Oh. Who from?

JACK: A mate.

EMMA: Anyone I know?

JACK: No. Just a mate.

EMMA: *(Pause)* He's leaving today, isn't he?

JACK: Who?

EMMA: Liam.

JACK: *(Feigning surprise)* Oh, yeah.

EMMA: Starts his new job at the weekend, he said.

JACK: That's right.

EMMA: It's funny. We never got that drink in. You know, the *three* of us.

JACK: That was Sarah's fault. Her turning up like that.

EMMA: And every time I rang he was always out somewhere. Sometimes they said he was up here.

JACK: Yeah. Tidying up the garden, most likely.

EMMA: At half eight at night?

JACK: I know he was sorting out the shed. Checking out the tools and that.

EMMA: *(Ironically)* Well there's devotion!

JACK: And saying his goodbyes, I suppose.

EMMA: Yeah, that'll be it. Still, I'm sure he'll be back from time to time.

JACK: Yeah. Bound to be. Anyway, Em, I'll give you a ring later. You know . . . if I change my mind. I've got a bit of college work to do. Either that or we'll meet in the week.

EMMA: *(Kisses him on the cheek)* Okay. You take care now.

JACK: Bye. *(Emma leaves).* *(To himself)* Take care of what?

(Jack picks up his book of Pond Maintenance. Sarah sees Emma leave but Emma does not see her.)

SCENE 19

(Sarah's house. The doorbell rings)

JACK: I'll go.

SARAH: It's okay.

(Jack goes to answer it. Enter Jane.)

JACK: Oh, it's you.

(They look at each other for a moment)

JANE: Hello to you too, Jack. Were you expecting someone else?

JACK: No, no. Sorry. I was in the middle of working.

JANE: There was *such* expectancy on your face!

JACK: Oh?

JANE: Sarah says you've been quite busy lately.

JACK: Yes. Yes, I have. *(Enter Sarah)*

SARAH: Hello, Jane.

JANE: Hi.

(Jack leaves. They sit down)

SARAH: Can I get you a cup of tea?

JANE: No. I'm fine. *(Pause)* Are you okay, though?

SARAH: Yes. I'm all right.

JANE: I was meaning after our little nocturnal adventure.

SARAH: Yes. *(Pause)* Emma was here, by the way.

JANE: Emma?

SARAH: Came to see Jack. Cool as anything.

JANE: Aha.

SARAH: I didn't say anything. I knew she was downstairs. I just kept out of the way.

JANE: No. Well, perhaps it's better not to.

SARAH: I was feeling so *angry.*

JANE: I see.

SARAH: Angry for Jack.

JANE: Well . . . . *(Doorbell rings)* Shall I go?

SARAH: No. It's okay.

(She goes to answer it. Off-stage voices. Jane gazes round the room.
Enter Liam. He is cheerful, smiling)

LIAM: Morning, all. *(Jack appears)* Jane.

JANE: Hello, Liam. *(Pause)* Today's the big day, then?

LIAM: Certainly is. Anyway, I thought I'd just pop in to say goodbye.

(Nods to Jack. Jack acknowledges him)

SARAH: What time are you leaving, Liam?

LIAM: I've got a train at two.

JANE: You must be raring to go. Mind you, you look a bit tired, though.

LIAM: *(Laughs)* You know how it is. Goodbye celebrations. *(Jack looks away)* Still, it's a challenge I'm looking forward to. Lots of work. But I'll miss my friends . . .

(Jack looks at him)

SARAH: *(Coldly)* Well, Emma'll miss you, for one. Won't she?

JANE: *(Intervenes)* What about your accommodation up there. Is that all paid for?

LIAM: I'll be living in, so yes.

JANE: That'll be quite a saving!

SARAH: Would you like anything to drink, Liam?

LIAM: Er. yes. I've got time for a quick one.

(Embarrassed silence)

JANE: Well, I'd better be off. I'll leave you to it.

SARAH: You're not staying?

JANE: No. I've got some work to do.

JACK: Yeah. Me too.

(Smiles at Liam. Jack leaves)

SARAH: I'll catch up with you later, Jane. I must say my goodbyes to
            our star gardener. *(Jane leaves)* Now, Liam. What would you
            like to drink?

LIAM: Er . . . A beer would be nice . . . if you've got any?

SARAH: I certainly have. I think I'll join you. We can drink to your
            future conquests.

LIAM: Pardon?

SARAH: Gardens, of course. What did you think I meant? *(They chink
            glasses)*

SCENE 20

(The pub. Emma sits at a table alone. She drinks a pint.
Mrs. Glass is putting away glasses. Jane enters)

JANE: Hello, Emma.

EMMA: Hi.

JANE: It's not often I get invites to the pub. Is something wrong?

EMMA: *(Looking towards Mrs. Glass. To Jane)* What would you like to drink?

JANE: Oh, er . . . a tomato juice.

EMMA: *(To Mrs. Glass)* A tomato juice, please.

MRS. GLASS: Worcester sauce?

JANE: Yes, please.

EMMA: And I'll have another half, Mrs. G.

(Mrs. Glass passes drinks. They sit down away from the bar)

JANE: So, Emma. What is it you wanted to talk about?

EMMA: Well, you might think I'm being silly but I just wondered if I'd done anything to . . . well, upset Sarah . . . Mrs. Medlock.

JANE: Upset? How do you mean?

EMMA: Well, if she was angry with me over something? Something
           I've done?

JANE: What makes you say that?

EMMA: The other day she was in here with some friends and, as I went
           past, she just looked right through me. Not a word. Nothing.

JANE: She did? You weren't here with Jack, were you? You know she
           disapproves of . . .

EMMA: No, no. I wasn't. I was with some lads from the village.

JANE: Maybe it was a bit noisy and . . .

EMMA: No, it wasn't like that. We passed her on the way out into the
           garden. Phil wanted to have a fag, so when I saw her I said
           hello and she just said nothing.

JANE: Perhaps she didn't see you. Especially if she was busy talking.

EMMA: No, she *saw* me all right! It was the same the other day when I
           went to call for Jack. He's been acting strange lately, too. Gone
           all reclusive. Anyway, I said hello but she didn't react. She was
           talking away to the new gardener, that long-haired bloke. Just
           ignored me. I think *he* noticed.

JANE: She's got a new gardener?

EMMA: Yes. Someone called Danny, according to Jack.

JANE: That's quick. She didn't tell *me*. I suppose she's keen for someone
           to carry on the good work. It *is* looking very impressive. That
           boy has worked wonders.

EMMA: Anyway, so I just wondered if I'd done anything to upset her.
           Whether she'd said anything. Or she'd seen Jack and me in
           here.

JANE: No, Emma, she hasn't, or she would have mentioned it.

EMMA: Well, I don't know why . . .

JANE: Emma, I'm sure it's nothing *you've* done.

EMMA: You think so?

JANE: Yes, really. It's been a difficult time. You know, with Leo. Not coming back and all that. But you're *really* not to blame.

EMMA: I was quite worried.

JANE: And then there's Liam.

EMMA: What about him?

JANE: Sarah was quite fond of him. Giving support at a difficult time.

EMMA: Is that what she told you?

JANE: Yes. And now he's gone, so it's bound to be a difficult time.

EMMA: *(Pause)* Thanks, Jane. That's the worst thing, really.

JANE: What is?

EMMA: Not knowing. Not knowing the real reason.

JANE: She's always been a bit moody has Sarah. She's sometimes like that with me. Things haven't been easy.

(Enter Jack. Jane sees him. For a moment, Jack appears to retreat. Jane downs drink. Jane and Jack look at each other for a moment or two. Each seems partly paralysed.)

Ah, here's Jack. I'll leave you to it. And don't worry.

(Motioning towards Jack to join them)

I won't say anything to Sarah. She'll never know. I won't say anything.

(Blackout)

SWIFTS

First performed on 21 November 2004 at the Chocolate Factory,
North London under the direction of Dimitri Devdariani.

CAST LIST

Richard

Anne

James—Anne's Brother

First, Second, Third Chorus Member

(Stage. One chair, spotlight. Richard comes to sit on chair)

(Pause)

(He looks up)

RICHARD: You asked me, didn't you? Asked me about where I first met them? *(Pause)* It was during the long hot summer. Yes, that's right. *(Pause)* Quite ironic that it should prove so productive, but yes, it was during those endless weeks of drought. *(Pause)* I first saw them on the pier.

(String of coloured lights lit up. Sound of sea. Richard gets up walks slowly along the pier. Looks out to sea. Couple approach. Richard turns round, glances quickly at them then addresses audience)

RICHARD: I was walking round like you do, looking at the sea between the slats, frothing, bubbling. And then I saw her face under a ring of those coloured light bulbs. It was slowly getting dark, but there was still the last of the sunset which hadn't yet vanished behind the cliff. They both looked very young—and so they were, of course. Those eyes, those pale blue eyes. They sparkled in the lights. *(Laughter can be heard)* In the distance, the church tower loomed up, watching us, adding its blessing. They go in for those tall church towers round here. Used to act as lookouts too. *(They leave the pier, Richard follows. They abruptly turn and exit.* I remember swifts screaming and flying low. *(Sound of swifts. Pause)* Now these birds . . . Did you know they do everything on the wing? Eat, sleep—seldom land. They fly like little sickles, half-question marks across the sky. *(Short pause, he sits down, says to the air)* You're beautiful . . .

(Pause again, he sinks in his thoughts)

Far beyond the amber glass and the sighing, shifting sea, those eyes imprinted themselves on me, and I heard her laugh once again.

(Sound of sea)

RICHARD'S BEDROOM

*(Richard lying on bed motionless, then gradually stirs.
Looks at clock then rushes, gets up to address audience)*

RICHARD: The next day, the rains came. A sullen drizzle and a sea mist.
The town as empty and deserted as if an unexploded bomb
had drifted up on the beach.

*(Anxious chorus of "bomb". Richard looks a little irritated at the off-stage chorus.
Scene now moves to Lifeboat Café)*

RICHARD: But on the Saturday, in the Lifeboat Café—I believe, I really
believe fate struck.

(Anne sits down at the next table)

FIRST CHORUS PERSON: Quick !
SECOND CHORUS PERSON: Get a line. Seize the moment!
THIRD CHORUS PERSON: *(To the First and Second Chorus
Person)* Throw a line to a drowning man!

RICHARD: *(To Anne)* Could you pass the salt ? *(She passes a pot of salt to
him)*   Thank you. *(Richard uses it and passes it back. Anne
gets up as if she is ready to go. Richard looks alarmed. She goes to a*

counter and orders another cup of tea. He sits back, more relaxed now. Short pause)

RICHARD: The seagulls were flying out after the fishing boats. Have you noticed that herring gulls have a nasty laugh? That is when they're not screeching across the harbours. *(Anne comes back and suddenly lurches forward. She showers Richard in tea)*

ANNE: Oh, I'm so sorry.

RICHARD: No, no. It's okay. No damage done. *(Richard wipes tea from white flannels)*

ANNE: It's these stupid legs. *(Hesitates)* I mean the table, not mine.

RICHARD: It's okay, don't worry about it. Here let me get you another tea.

ANNE: It's okay. The cup's still half-full.

RICHARD: An optimist, eh?

ANNE: Sorry? Oh, I see . . . half-full.

RICHARD: Did you come here before?

ANNE: No, never. Just drew out a map, stuck in a pin and here we are.

(Pause)

RICHARD: It's beautiful coast.

ANNE: We're going back on Friday. James works weekends.

RICHARD: James?

ANNE: My brother.

RICHARD: Oh, what does he do?

ANNE: In a hospital. Porter. It's important that we get back. He's tried loads of jobs but none of them really suited him. Except this one. He quite likes . . .

(They talk but the sound is drowned out by the sea washing over pebbles. James enters the café. Looks round)

ANNE: What kept you?

JAMES: Left my sunglasses in the pub, didn't I?

ANNE: *(To Richard)* He's always leaving things behind. Nearly always in pubs too.

JAMES: Means you have to go back next day.

RICHARD: *(To Anne)* Do you like pubs? I mean, we could go for a drink before you go back.

ANNE: Yes, that's a good idea. Tomorrow?

JAMES: *(Laughs)* Suits me

RICHARD: Tomorrow it is then.

(They stand outside first pub)

ANNE: Oh, I don't know. It looks a bit crowded.

(They trudge on)

RICHARD: How about this one?

ANNE: *(In trepidation)* Looks a bit smoky.

(They trudge on to Pub 3)

ANNE: Oh lots of comatose old men.

JAMES: Looks like my hospital ward. What about this one? *(He points)*
               We could sit outside.

RICHARD: And so we did. Quaffing pints as the tide began to turn,
               dragging across the beach, buffeting the pier. *(To audience)* I
               looked into those beautiful eyes and was hypnotised.

AT THE RAILWAY STATION

ANNE: I can't believe a week's gone so quickly.

JAMES: *(To Anne)* Look! Your cheeks are glowing.

ANNE: *(Excitedly)* The air's so fresh up here. So invigorating.

JAMES: Nonsense, it's all that drinking. Honestly, she doesn't normally drink that much.

RICHARD: Let me give you my address and you write yours.

(They exchange tiny bits of paper. While they do so members of the Chorus comment on it)

FIRST CHORUS PERSON: *(To audience)* Little bits of precious paper . . .

SECOND CHORUS PERSON: He would write.

THIRD CHORUS PERSON: They would meet up.

ALL THREE: He would make sure of it!

(Richard kisses Anne on both cheeks. James squeezes his arm. They enter the train)

RICHARD'S BEDROOM

(Richard walks slowly to table. Writes slowly and seals envelope. Lies down on bed and waits. Variety of positions on bed)

(Letter flies through the air—lands on mat. Richard rushes to pick it up. Looks and smiles to audience)

RICHARD: A letter. You can see. A letter. She had written. Little spidery writing. Amoebas crossing the page. Then they came more frequently.

(Many letters are flung at Richard)

And of course I wrote. *(Picks up one red envelope)* Yes!
(Mouths delight) "Come and see us" *(Rushes to pick up suitcase)*

TRAIN

(Comes downstage holding model train)

RICHARD: Marshes to the east. Marshes west. Marshes everywhere. The train swaying in a breezy emptiness.

(Pause)

I nearly missed the station. Small and apologetic—a wooden hut for shelter. A ticket office long abandoned.

(Richard looks at departing train. Silence. Momentarily panics. James emerges on the platform)

JAMES: She's stood you up.
RICHARD: What?
JAMES: *(Smiles)* Playing tennis, so she sent me to pick you up. Some sort of knockout tournament.
JAMES: Fancy a drink? Celebrate your arrival.
RICHARD: Sure, why not? *(They start walking)* There's nothing but reeds in this place.
JAMES: And water. Water everywhere. The pub's round the next bend.

(Two beers appear on table. James drinks and belches)

FIRST CHORUS PERSON: *(To audience)* As they sat outside the pub, he noticed how white his teeth were.

JAMES: *(Gazing at beer)* This is why I didn't take the car. Would you like another one?

RICHARD: This beer is very heady. I feel already quite . . . *(Smiling)* Unco-ordi-nated.

JAMES: That's all right, you can stay a long weekend, if you wish.

(They laugh. James gets two beers. They drink)

(Pause.)

RICHARD: So, do you enjoy it, the job you do?

JAMES: *(Pause)* Yes, yes. I suppose I do. *(Pause)* Mind you, work is very over-rated.

RICHARD: Over-rated?

JAMES: Yes, over-rated. And very inconvenient at times . . . Interferes with your social life, no end.

RICHARD: *(Laughs)* How long have you been doing it?

JAMES: The hospital? Nearly two years. But all the time the place is getting smaller.

RICHARD: Smaller?

JAMES: Yes, well either the psychotics are getting miraculously cured, or else it's something to do with building on the land. *(Pause)* Tear down a hospital and build houses. That's logic for you.

RICHARD: Then what will you do?

JAMES: Wait and see. Move on. Try something else. The people in the new houses will be so astonishingly healthy, they won't need hospitals. *(James grins)*

RICHARD: And you've never been tempted by the City?. Business, banking?

JAMES: *(Nearly coughs into his glass)* Can you see me doing it? Selling things, I mean. All dressed up, all interested.

RICHARD: I dunno, maybe. Maybe not. We've all got to earn the crust.

JAMES: Well for the moment I'll settle for a few crumbs. Another pint?

(Sound of people playing tennis off stage. They stand up, abandoning their glasses. Ann enters with tennis racquets, gives each to her brother and Richard. Ann and James freeze with racquets in their hands. Richard continues narration, playing with his racquet, looking at it with curiosity, so that it's clear that he is not a very experienced player)

RICHARD: Played tennis every day. Found muscles I didn't know existed. I tried my hand at canoeing. Canoed down the river Ant or the Slug or something.

(Canoe appears slowly then Richard yells and freezes)

Nearly garrotted by overhanging trees. They tenderly extricated me from the advances of willow. (Brushing off the leaves and stray bits of bark. They extricate him as described) Came back most weekends and was garrotted some more.

LONDON

(Anne arrives. Steps off train. They kiss)

RICHARD: And so, one day in late autumn, leaves falling from trees. *(Single leaf falls)* We tied the knot. Little café near Holborn Circus. Words nearly drowned by the Espresso machine. *(Sound of Espresso machine)*

(Pause)

ANNE: *(Excited on phone)* Hello, yes. Yes, it's me. Yes, everything is fine. Well it's more than fine. I've got some news. Yes, you know. The one I met on holiday. We've been seeing a lot of . . . Yes, going to get married. No, we haven't set a date. Yes. Will you tell James or shall I? Ok . . . yes, yes I'll tell him . . . Yes, right away . . . Thank you . . . Yes, I will. *(Clasps receiver happily to her cheek)*

FIRST CHORUS PERSON: Then she made another call to tell James. He was rambling in the Lake District. Buttermere. She had to tell him too.

SECOND CHORUS PERSON: It was always like that. Instinctively thought about each other. Reflex action. Like mirror twins—except they weren't.

THIRD CHORUS PERSON: She returned beaming after making the calls.

(Anne beams)

RICHARD: We went to a restaurant to celebrate. Groomed spinach accompanied by paltry potatoes and lamb resting poignantly on 3 leaves of cress.

We should have stayed in the café and blown up with lasagne.

(Pause)
(Anne puts away an elegant restaurant dish and picks up a cornflake-bowl, eats slowly)

RICHARD: Are you okay? You've hardly eaten . . . *(Anne drops spoon)* What's up?

ANNE: Travelling. It's the travelling. It's getting me down. So long on the train and then the bus. I don't think I'm cut out for big cities.

RICHARD: We don't have to stay here. I never thought of it as permanent.

ANNE: Do you mean that? I mean, you're not just saying that.

RICHARD: I don't mind. We can move . . . if you're not happy here. *(Pause)* Have you thought where?

ANNE: Not really . . . Just somewhere smaller. Anywhere.

RICHARD: Okay, then. Let's go anywhere.

RICHARD: *(To audience)* It worked quite well. We travelled less. Anne could do her stained glass stuff at home.

(Anne looks up)

ANNE: It's not stuff. *(Mock indignance)*

RICHARD: We cycled off to obscure pubs with unknown beers. *(They mime cycling simultaneously)* Roads that always went upwards whichever way you went and a biting wind that blew into you. Many a time we saved each other from lurking ditches as we meandered helplessly across the road.

JAMES: Help!

(Falls off road. Richard 'rescues' him. James leaves the stage)

ANNE: Do you know what next week is?

RICHARD: *(Thoughtfully)* Elections in Matabeleland? Your uncle's having a bunion lanced?

ANNE: *(Hits him with a book)* No!

RICHARD: Some kind of event? A commemoration perhaps?

ANNE: Try a little harder.

RICHARD: It's not, is it?

ANNE: *(Nods)* Our second anniversary.

RICHARD: Of course it is. *(Enthusiastically)* We should do something. Down tools and go away. A holiday.

ANNE: If you think I'm camping again . . .

RICHARD: But those bed and breakfasts!

ANNE: No way!

RICHARD: The fresh air when you wake up in a tent. It's so . . . *(Pause)* Okay, so where would you like to go?

ANNE: *(Looks at him knowingly)*

RICHARD: Where we first met? You softie, you old romantic!

FIRST CHORUS PERSON: *(To audience)* In fact the weather settled the argument regarding any camping Grey skies and chilly winds buried the atmosphere of balmy evenings.

SECOND CHORUS PERSON: The swifts had long gone, abandoning the summer, leaving the gulls to screech across the harbour.

RICHARD: Shame about the weather. It's so changeable. That's always the problem. The swifts have gone. What a pity.

ANNE: I don't mind. I don't mind. Just think if we'd been in a tent.

RICHARD: Tents are quite cosy really so long as you follow dietary precautions. I mean . . . *(Looks at Anne)* Okay, okay you were right.

(Richard puts his arms around her waist)

SECOND CHORUS PERSON*: (To audience)* He wondered whether she would want James to come but she made no mention.

(They walk along the beach, holding hands. Waves, gulls)

RICHARD: *(To audience)* We walked along the beaches most days, taking in the crisp sea air. Air so fresh it made you feel really alive. *(Pause)* One afternoon, we went for a longer walk and headed beyond the pier. Those beautiful eyes, I thought. Lonely stretches of sand tapering into nowhere. Constant ripples in grey sandpools. Looking out to sea, a mist was beginning to form and there was the distant sound of a foghorn . . . I looked behind us, but there was nothing but open beach and waves crashing against breakwaters.

(Pause)

We went up to the cliffs. The ground was still moist after the morning drizzle.

(Pause)

We trod paths that wound through bracken and gorse. I had no idea of the time but Anne kept looking at her watch.

(Pause)

Funny thing to do when you're at the sea . . . as she did . . . almost surreal.

(Pause)

We turned back, Anne walking slightly ahead on the narrow path. Birds scuttled across; low-flying and scolding. The mist brooded on the horizon.

(Pause)

You know, I can't really recall it. You know, when your mind goes blank sometimes. But I do remember the foghorn. That bleak,doleful sound.

(Pause and foghorn)

Just past the bend in the cliffpath, Anne had slipped. It may have been the wet stones or sudden subsidence. (brief pause). She was never that nimble on her feet.

(Everything vanishes. Spotlight on Richard)

Of course, everyone was sympathetic.

(Hands of chorus members firmly grasp his shoulders)

Sometimes painfully so.

(The hands disappear)

But between those long, staring silences, I had James all to myself . . . He would be in need of comfort . . . . Those beautiful eyes.

(Blackout)

NOT A WAVE VISIBLE
OR
AFTER CYRIL

CAST LIST

Ernest Hambleton—A Retired Pensioner

Hilda Jones—A Retired Pensioner

Irma

Eileen

Young Man

Young Woman

SCENE 1

(Seaside town. Shelter situated on a hill looking out to sea. Hilda Jones approaches the shelter slowly and comes and sits down. After a moment she takes something from her bag, looks at it and then puts it back. She gazes out to sea. The sound of herring gulls overhead. She looks to her right. Ernest Hambleton approaches the shelter, raises his hat and sits down)

ERNEST: Good morning, Mrs. Jones.

HILDA: Morning. *(Long pause)* Looks quite nice, doesn't it? At the moment, that is.

ERNEST: Always the way, isn't it?

HILDA: Is it, Mr. H?

ERNEST: It is. It gets warmer and then the clouds build up. Overcast, you see. But by the afternoon, it's rain.

HILDA: It's nice now, isn't it? *(She looks at him for reassurance)*

ERNEST: Yes, it is. *(Pause)* Well, good day to you, Mrs. Jones.

HILDA: What? Well, you're soon off. Where are you going?

ERNEST: The Sally Army shop's open. Might get a cup of tea.

HILDA: Is it Wednesday today?

ERNEST: All day, my dear.

HILDA: *(Looks puzzled)* What do you mean, all day? Is it Wednesday or isn't it?

ERNEST: It's just my little joke.

HILDA: Oh, I see. A joke. I've never been very good at those. It was my Cyril, you see. Never laughed. Come to think of it, never smiled much either. Sort of rubs off, I suppose.

ERNEST: I see.

HILDA: I suppose they do courses in that now at the new college.

ERNEST: Which new college?

HILDA: The one they built the other side of Pier Lane. You know, next to the park where the bowling green was.

ERNEST: Ah, that one. That's almost funny, Mrs. Jones. Courses on laughing. Very good.

HILDA: That's 'cos my Cyril ain't here. Mind you, I did read about it in the papers.

ERNEST: Read what?

HILDA: About laughing. It said in Sweden they were doing it.

ERNEST: I'm not surprised.

HILDA: Why's that, then?

ERNEST: Anyone who names themselves after a bland, dreary vegetable obviously needs cheering up.

HILDA: Do you think so? I sometimes cook 'em with a bit of fennel. Peps it up no end.

ERNEST: I do, Mrs. Jones.

HILDA: Maybe it isn't the same in Swedish. They probably call it something else.

ERNEST: I shouldn't think so. (Looks at his watch) Well, I can't sit around all day talking about vegetables. I'd better be off or I'll miss the tea.

HILDA: You don't want that, Mr. H. You don't want to miss yer tea.

ERNEST: Goodbye, Mrs. Jones.

HILDA: Goodbye, dear.

SCENE 2

(Hilda Jones walks slowly to the shelter. She sits down. Laughing sound of herring gull above. She looks up)

HILDA: *(To herself)* That sea is so still. It looks like a huge grey mirror. Nothing today. No wind. *(Pause)* Oh, I fancy some chocolate.

(Enter Ernest Hambleton)

ERNEST: What's that, Mrs. Jones?

HILDA: Ooh! *(Takes a deep breath)*

ERNEST: Are you okay?

HILDA: You startled me.

ERNEST: I heard you talking.

HILDA: Was I?

ERNEST: You were.

HILDA: I don't recall. I was just looking at the sea.

ERNEST: Very still today, isn't it?

HILDA: Nothing's moving.

ERNEST: It's like this place.

HILDA: *(Laughs)* That's a joke, isn't it? You know, you're quite humorous, Mr. H.

ERNEST: *(Stands up and bows)* Glad to be of service. *(Sits down)*

HILDA: What do you mean, it's like this place?

ERNEST: What I said. It's quiet here.

HILDA: It'll soon be July. Then the day-trippers'll be coming.

ERNEST: There's not as many, though, as there used to be. Have you noticed? They're probably on the Costa del Sol, or whatever it's called,

HILDA: Probably gone to Blackpool, more likely.

ERNEST: No, not now. It's buying houses in other countries. *(Pause)*

HILDA: It's no good, is it?

ERNEST: No good for what?

HILDA: Buying extra houses. They should be glad they've got one! Me and Cyril always rented. I'm in a Council flat off Beck Row, well, you know. Some years back, they asked us if we wanted to buy.

ERNEST: And did you?

HILDA: Cyril told them to bugger off.

ERNEST: Not in as many words, surely?

HILDA: They was his exact words. He was on the telephone.

ERNEST: So you have a telephone?

HILDA: That took years of resistance which I had to overcome. He says, 'there's a phone box across the green. We can use that if we have to.' I says, 'what if you're ill, you great pillock and that box isn't working. You expect me to go traipsing across town!'

ERNEST: What did he say?

HILDA: Nothing. He knew he was stumped. Argument disinty . . . something.

ERNEST: Grating.

HILDA: That's it. Thank you. So I says, 'no. I'll go to a neighbour's and make a call from there.' That was my trump card. He wasn't having any of that. Didn't really like the neighbours, did Cyril. So we had a phone within a week.

ERNEST: Good for you! It's not a luxury, it's a necessity nowadays.

HILDA: Especially when the public ones is always broken. I never liked that one across the green anyway. Mr. Bartram used to pop in there for a wee.

ERNEST: How disgusting!

HILDA: Used to make out he was reading the phone book but I knew what he was doing. Then they started painting them boxes different colours. I walked past them half the time.

ERNEST: Red is a more sensible colour, I feel.

HILDA: It's disappearing, though. Look at the buses. All shapes and sizes now. Missed one the other week because it was the wrong colour. *(Pause)* I'm told the Chinese like it. And the Russians.

ERNEST: You're a mine of information, Mrs. Jones. Where do you get all this?

HILDA: I listen to the radio. These things come up. Cyril never used to let me listen. There was a four letter word on the radio, one day . . . and he cut the plug off.

ERNEST: I'm amazed! Is there a country you don't know about?

HILDA: Now you're being silly, Mr. H!

ERNEST: What about the Koreans?

HILDA: They eat cats *(Pause)* and maybe dogs, too. I'm not quite sure
            about that.

ERNEST: That's not a bad idea, you know. Some of the ones round here
            would keep you going for weeks.

HILDA: You can't eat them!

ERNEST: My neighbour, Mrs. Bridywell, well, hers is the size of a small
            leopard. It sleeps all day. Can't even climb the stairs. Hasn't
            caught a mouse for years.

HILDA: It doesn't need to.

ERNEST: Well, it couldn't even if it wanted to. You know, cats are the
            most amazing things. If you had a house guest that slept
            around all day and didn't do a stroke of work, well you'd soon
            show them the door, wouldn't you? But not with this lot. On
            the contrary. We welcome them in.

HILDA: It is still today, isn't it?

ERNEST: Pardon?

HILDA: Look around you. Not a breath of wind.

ERNEST: At least it's not raining.

HILDA: I wouldn't mind if it did. That way there's something going
            on. *(Pause)* You know what's wrong with this place, Mr. H?

ERNEST: No.

HILDA: There's too many old people.

SCENE 3

(Ernest Hambleton is sitting in the shelter. Mrs. Jones approaches.)

ERNEST: Good morning to you, Mrs. Jones. *(He stands up and raises his hat)*

HILDA: *(Stops to regain her breath)* Ooh!

ERNEST: Are you all right, Mrs. Jones?

HILDA: Yes, yes. I'm all right. It's that hill. It gets steeper every time. And my legs feel like putty. As if they're not moving at all.

ERNEST: But the reward is the view.

HILDA: I suppose so. That's if you could see anything.

ERNEST: Sea fret.

HILDA: It's certainly sea fret, all right. Do you remember, about four years ago? The sea mist came in and lasted over three weeks.

ERNEST: I do indeed. It was a source of great frustration.

HILDA: It just wouldn't go. Wouldn't budge. And yet everywhere across the country was basking in hot temperatures . . .

ERNEST: So I'm told.

HILDA: My daughter Jean took me in to Birchington. She wanted me to look at a laundry basket. I couldn't concentrate. That store was too hot.

ERNEST: And the place you wanted to be . . .

HILDA:	Was beside the sea. Only we was covered in that mist.
ERNEST:	That's the problem with high pressure.
HILDA:	Oh no. I didn't have any problems then.
ERNEST:	I meant the weather, Mrs. Jones. High pressure. It doesn't change. We were stuck under a blanket of low cloud.
HILDA:	*(Interrupts)* We got company, Mr. H.
ERNEST:	Pardon?
HILDA:	*(Jerks her thumb)* The next shelter.
ERNEST:	Next shelter? Oh, I see.
HILDA:	It's that lad who works Saturday down the supermarket.
ERNEST:	Which supermarket?
HILDA:	The one at Beeston Cross.
ERNEST:	I never go there. Not if I can help it. I make two trips to the Saturday market. Buy all my fruit and veg there. Fruit in the morning. Veg after lunch.
HILDA:	Why two trips?
ERNEST:	I can't carry it all. Besides, I like the walk. I go through the avenue and along the park. And when I come home I take the quicker way back.
HILDA:	*(Ignoring him)* I wonder who the other lad is. He looks like his brother.
ERNEST:	Have you noticed, Mrs. Jones, that the people who sit in these shelters are either the very old or the very young? There's nothing in between.
HILDA:	That's 'cos they're all working. And less of the very old.
ERNEST:	I should say elderly, of course.
HILDA:	No, you can say old. There's nothing wrong in that.

ERNEST: You're quite right, Mrs. Jones. But I'm afraid to say nowadays there's no association with dignity. Words like old fool, codger.

HILDA: Well, you can't have a young codger, can you? Come to think of it, you can't have a codger at all. You've got to have old.

ERNEST: That's my point. It's become a term of abuse. A simple word like that.

HILDA: But not in China, it ain't. Or Japan. They respect old people.

ERNEST: Really, Mrs. Jones? The radio, I suppose?

HILDA: A travel programme on the telly. I'd nearly dozed off and . . .

ERNEST: Full of information. Quite remarkable.

HILDA: The presenter was quite tasty. *(She points)* Bit like that lad there. *(Long pause)* Do you feel old, Mr. H?

ERNEST: I beg your pardon, Mrs. Jones?

HILDA: What I said. Do you consider yourself as old?

ERNEST: Well . . . .

HILDA: It's a simple question.

ERNEST: Parts of my body do, but my head.

HILDA: Your head?

ERNEST: Yes, well, my mind . . . what I feel inside, then, no.

HILDA: That's what I meant. Me too, I suppose. I mean, them two lads. The taller one's quite good looking.

ERNEST: Mrs. Jones! At your age!

HILDA: That's what I was saying. If I was younger I could really . . .

ERNEST: What are they doing now?

HILDA: The younger one's swinging from the roof.

ERNEST: I need my glasses. *(Puts them on)* Well . . . the little vandal!

HILDA: He's just showing off. Excess energy, I imagine.

ERNEST: I wouldn't be surprised if the guttering came down.

HILDA: Now he's turning round . . . one hand. Nice body. Not as good as his brother, though.

ERNEST: I don't know. Ah. Now I can see. I would say he's better, Mrs. Jones. He has the most beautiful, firm bottom.

HILDA: He has.

ERNEST: It's a work of art. It's quite unusual now. Most of them wear these ghastly baggy things that hang down to their kneecaps. Looks highly unpleasant.

HILDA: Awful.

ERNEST: Most depressing. It means the joy of arse is quite forgotten. But this boy is certainly special.

HILDA: See, if only we were younger. It isn't fair.

ERNEST: Oh! Oh, I'm so sorry, Mrs. Jones! What was I saying?

HILDA: You were admiring that young man's bottom. The joy of arse, I think you said.

ERNEST: Did I really? I'm so sorry. I completely forgot myself.

HILDA: No, no, Mr. H. I think you remembered yourself.

ERNEST: Remembered myself? How?

HILDA: You saw something beautiful—well, you thought it was and I thought it's not bad either—and you weren't afraid to say it.

ERNEST: You're not shocked?

HILDA: Why should I be? *(Pause)* Times has changed. People talk about it now.

ERNEST: I suppose this is your post-Cyril liberation, Mrs. Jones.

HILDA: I shouldn't be asking this but were you married, Mr. H?

ERNEST: Yes, yes, I was.

HILDA: Were you happy?

ERNEST: I never stopped to think. But yes, in a way, I think I was.

HILDA: And did you like young men then?

ERNEST: Very much.

HILDA: But you got married?

ERNEST: It was the done thing. Expected of you. And I've always been good at doing the done thing. I suppose it suited me well enough. But passion . . .

HILDA: What about it?

ERNEST: It was never really there. Sometimes a flicker.

HILDA: A flicker?

ERNEST: A candle in the wind.

HILDA: Oh.

ERNEST: It was usually after I went to cricket.

HILDA: Oh yes, the old ground. They built on it, didn't they?

ERNEST: A supermarket. Blocked off my sole escape route. Of an afternoon sometimes, in that siesta period after lunch, I'd get talking. A young lad on his own.

HILDA: At the cricket?

ERNEST: It would just make me feel good. To be with someone young again. Someone who saw things differently. Then, for some reason, I'd want to buy them something. To show my gratitude. An ice cream or a drink perhaps. And I'd go back home feeling as if the sun had shone on me all day.

HILDA: It's tiring going to cricket. All that fresh air. I got sunburnt once.

ERNEST: I'd hardly ever see them again. They'd perhaps be there for the one day. I'd look for them but they'd never show. *(Pause)* Sometimes I think they were avoiding me.

HILDA: Avoiding you. Why would they do that?

ERNEST: There was one lad, Steven. He was down for a week staying with his aunt and uncle. Nice looking lad. They were at work during the day, so he went off to the cricket. No one at home, you see. And I thought, if he were mine . . . my nephew, I mean, well, I'd be so proud. I'd look after him, seeing as it was his holiday. I'd be proud to be his uncle; seeing that we're of the same blood.

HILDA: Yes. That's very poetic.

ERNEST: I went to the same cricket week, same time of year, but he wasn't there. I looked forward to it for months. Months of expectation. But he never showed. Maybe it wasn't much fun for him. Or perhaps it was a one off. The lack of hospitality might have . . . .

HILDA: *(Looks towards the shelter. She gives a gasp)* The other one tried it and nearly fell off. *(They look for a moment. She laughs)* I suppose if he was injured, I could rush forward and give him the kiss of life.

ERNEST: He might have a relapse. *(Laughs)* Besides, there'd be stiff competition.

HILDA: That's not very nice, Mr. H. After all you've been saying.

ERNEST: I didn't think you were listening.

HILDA: You stick to your one and I'll stick to mine.

ERNEST: If only . . .

HILDA:　　　Only?

ERNEST:　　We were younger.

HILDA:　　　That's right, Mr H. One each. If only.

SCENE 4

(Elderly woman at shelter, Irma. Mrs. Jones approaches slowly.
They nod to each other.)

HILDA: Oh, this hill.

IRMA: It's a bit of a trek, isn't it?

HILDA: I do it most days.

IRMA: Good exercise, I reckon.

HILDA: Pulls on me knees a bit. Mr. H says it quite wears him out.

IRMA: Mr. H?

HILDA: A friend. We often meet up here. You know, chat. Look out at the sea.

IRMA: There's plenty of it today.

HILDA: Is there? Of what?

IRMA: Sea. See how clear it is. You can see miles.

HILDA: So you can. I hadn't noticed. I was too busy climbing that hill. Mr. H enjoys the view. Always comments on it. Likes looking out. I can't think why he's not here today.

IRMA: Mr. H?

HILDA: Yes. His name's Ernest. But I always call him Mr. H. Looks like an aitch somehow. *(Irma laughs)* Why are you laughing?

IRMA: It just sounds funny. Was funny.

HILDA:	I'm making up for lost time.
IRMA:	I'm sorry?
HILDA:	It was my Cyril, see. When we was married, we didn't have no jokes. Very few. And if we did, he couldn't understand them. I had to spend weeks explaining them. Had to give up most of the time.
IRMA:	I couldn't have a man with no sense of humour. No, that's no good. Or a mean one.
HILDA:	He could be that too. Hated buying anything he did.
IRMA:	And Cyril?
HILDA:	He was run over in Blackpool by a tram. I always said he needed a new pair of glasses. I think he wasn't expecting a tram. Thought they'd all been done away with.
IRMA:	It must have been very traumatic for you.
HILDA:	Not really. I was down here. Mind you, I never found out what he was doing in Blackpool. I never asked. And then when I could have . . . *(Rubs her knee)*
IRMA:	*(Solicitously)* Arthritis, is it?
HILDA:	Always plays up in the hot weather. I don't understand it.
IRMA:	It's often the way. *(Pause)*
HILDA:	I don't think he'll come today. He's usually here by now.
IRMA:	And he has aches and pains too?
HILDA:	From time to time. Says he mustn't eat tomatoes. *(Pause)*
IRMA:	*(Suddenly)* How would you like to go to a dinner?
HILDA:	A dinner?
IRMA:	Yes.
HILDA:	What kind of dinner?

IRMA: Good honest, wholesome cooking. A lady who lives over Mile End way. Fabulous food. Uses herbs and things. And you know, after you've been for two or three meals, those aches and pains simply disappear.

HILDA: Do they really? That would be wonderful. Are you sure?

IRMA: I'm the proof. *(Points to her shoe)* This foot used to give me gyp sometimes, but now . . .

HILDA: You think it's the dinners?

IRMA: Must be. Haven't tried anything else. Nothing else has changed. They say it's all diet anyway.

HILDA: Well . . . I don't know. I'll think about it.

IRMA: You won't regret it.

HILDA: I'll mention it to Mr. H.

IRMA: Yes, you do that, my dear. It's good to have an escort.

SCENE 5

(The next day. Mr. Hambleton, Mrs. Jones)

HILDA: Good morning, Mr. H.

ERNEST: Good morning to you.

HILDA: We missed you yesterday.

ERNEST: It's a funny thing but I was just going out and I had this young man knocking at the door.

HILDA: Oh. Pensions, was it?

ERNEST: No. Canvassing.

HILDA: Oh. *(Pause)* Which party was it?

ERNEST: You know, I can't honestly remember.

HILDA: He was that good, eh?

ERNEST: As a matter of fact . . .

HILDA: That's nice.

ERNEST: I was all ears and quite forgot the time.

HILDA: Well, you would, wouldn't you?

ERNEST: Pity. It was such a beautiful day.

HILDA: You could see well out into the bay.

ERNEST: Pity . . .

HILDA: We sat here for some time.

ERNEST: We?

HILDA: Irma.

ERNEST: And who is Irma?

HILDA: An oldie just like us. We got talking.

ERNEST: I thought you said you weren't an oldie, Mrs. Jones.

HILDA: *(Ignoring him)* We got onto aches and pains. Niggly knees and the like. She gave me a telephone number.

ERNEST: Whatever for?

HILDA: Well, if you sit down, I'll tell you about it.

(MUSICAL INTERLUDE)

SCENE 6

(A street. Mr. Hambleton. Mrs. Jones)

ERNEST: Are you sure you have the correct address, Mrs. Jones? It doesn't look very promising.

HILDA: It depends what you're expecting. She's an old dear like us. She's hardly likely to live in a mansion.

ERNEST: *(Irritably)* Let me look again.

HILDA: I don't know. Our first time out together, away from the sea shelter and it's turning into a full blown row.

ERNEST: I wouldn't say that, Mrs. Jones. If you hadn't taken the wrong turning at the bottom, we wouldn't be here now.

HILDA: Well, if that was the case, why didn't you tell me?

ERNEST: I didn't want to interfere. You can so easily dent someone's confidence. Put them off. No, it would have been most unhelpful

HILDA: And what are you doing now?

ERNEST: Well, because it's plainly wrong.

HILDA: 48c, it says.

ERNEST: And this is 48.

HILDA: Let's go round this path. See where it goes.

ERNEST: But that's someone's garden, Mrs.Jones!

HILDA: Well, we won't find out, if we don't try. There was a man down the road. Why didn't we ask him?

ERNEST: At that time I felt there was no need.

HILDA: Typical!

ERNEST: What do you mean, typical?

HILDA: Typical man! Won't ever ask for directions.

ERNEST: The path, Mrs. Jones, is leading towards someone's rubbish bins.

HILDA: I'll put your irritation down to your arthritis, Ernest. *(Pause)*

ERNEST: What did you say? You called me Ernest.

HILDA: It's a new situation.

ERNEST: Situation! You've never used that word before.

HILDA: Time for change, I suppose.

ERNEST: I'm very surprised.

HILDA: Listen. I can hear voices. *(Pointing)* There's another house behind. *(They approach the building slowly. Ernest rings the bell. Mrs. Eileen Clegworth opens the door.)*

EILEEN: Ah, come in, my dears. We've been expecting you. *(Sounds of dinner guests chatting and laughing.)* You're both in for a treat.

SCENE 7

(On the doorstep of Eileen's house. Ernest, Hilda and Eileen.)

HILDA: Thank you, Eileen. That was a lovely evening. I haven't had food like that before . . .

ERNEST: It certainly was, my dear.

HILDA: Looks like we're the last to leave. We must be keeping you from . . . .

EILEEN: Not at all.

HILDA: At least let us wash up.

EILEEN: I wouldn't hear of it. People who come here for the first time are always the last to leave.

HILDA: Really?

ERNEST: Those cakes, Eileen. They were superb. Mouthwatering.

HILDA: Lovely.

ERNEST: So light. They simply melted in your mouth.

EILEEN: Everybody likes my cakes.

ERNEST: Now, Eileen, if you don't mind me asking, what is it in your food that is plainly so good for arthritis?

EILEEN: Just natural ingredients. You haven't felt the effects yet.

ERNEST: Can't say I have but I do feel wonderfully relaxed. And calm.

HILDA: Yes, calm. Simply serene.

ERNEST: And I seem to be picking up every sound. Every smell of the night air.

EILEEN: That'll be the honeysuckle wafting . . .

HILDA: It's a lovely evening.

ERNEST: All your guests swore by it. Says those suppers do the trick. *(Turning slightly)* Ah, I see you have a greenhouse.

EILEEN: I'm just glad to be of help. I mean, why suffer and keep a stiff upper lip when there's a way out?

HILDA: Exactly.

ERNEST: She's so wise, isn't she, Hilda?

HILDA: Ernest!

ERNEST: Yes, my dear.

HILDA: You've never called me Hilda before.

ERNEST: Have I not?

HILDA: No.

ERNEST: Perhaps I'm a little confused.

HILDA: Oh.

ERNEST: As you said, so aptly, out of context. A new environment. The sweet, sweet night air.

EILEEN: And now before you both go, I'd like to give you something in accordance with your wishes.

ERNEST: Our wishes?

EILEEN: Yes, yes. Come along. Something you both agreed on when you were at your usual meeting place.

ERNEST: Our usual meeting place? How would you know that?

EILEEN: You told me earlier. Don't you remember? And you were complaining about the hill.

HILDA: But we didn't mention no wishes.

EILEEN: *(Tapping her nose)* Trust me. It's all about trust. *(Goes over to another tin. Opens it with a loud noise as lid falls on the floor.)*

ERNEST: I don't think I could eat any more cake, Eileen. I'm blissfully full.

HILDA: *(Breathes in)* Heavenly! So am I, my dear.

EILEEN: This is my cake for special occasions, My wiya-wiya cake.

HILDA: If you say so.

EILEEN: I only make it once a year on account of its special properties. Whoever eats it can only eat it once too. Fulfilment guaranteed.

ERNEST: I'm certainly full, but your culinary skills, Eileen, are quite stupendous.

EILEEN: Think nothing of it. Now a small piece each! *(Ernest and Hilda both eat)*

ERNEST and HILDA: Oh, so delicious! How do you do it?

EILEEN: Aha! I'll say goodnight, then. Good luck and have fun!

ERNEST: Sheer wizardry! See you at the next dinner.

EILEEN: Undoubtedly. I'll see you both to the corner. It's a little dark and you might fall over the dustbins.

SCENE 8

(Young woman combs her hair. She hums as she does it and laughs.)

SCENE 9

(Young man also does his hair. He hums a little too, but more purposefully and briskly. When he's finished, he rubs his hands together)

SCENE 10

(The shelter. Young woman, young man)

WOMAN: It's a beautiful day! The sun is sparkling on the waves. And all around me, birdsong and the smell of cut grass. *(Young man approaches. He smiles)*

MAN: Hello.

WOMAN: Out walking?

MAN: Yes. I got up early and thought what's the point in sitting around? I should be out there.

WOMAN: Quite right. Me too. I hate to be cooped up on days like this. *(Lets out a chicken cluck)* Oh, I'm so sorry. I don't know what came over me.

MAN: That's no problem. Think nothing of it. I barked in the student canteen once.

WOMAN: You were a student?

MAN: Yes, I think so.

WOMAN: What were you studying?

MAN: I can't remember. It seems so long ago. I used to drink a lot of ale, though.

WOMAN: That's what studying's for. *(Pause)* Beer. I love beer. I used to live opposite a brewery.

MAN: A bit inconvenient, wasn't it?

WOMAN: Far from it. I dreamed every night I was down the pub. I saved a fortune.

MAN: What happened to it?

WOMAN: I spent it all on beer. The brewery closed and my dreams disappeared. Then they put a supermarket where it used to be in the neo-toilet style.

MAN: Neo-toilet? That's a new one on me.

WOMAN: Look closely and you'll see I'm right.

MAN: I will.

WOMAN: I cried every night the first week the brewery closed.

MAN: What happened next?

WOMAN: I think I got married.

MAN: You think?

WOMAN: It's not very clear. Surly bastard. I can't remember everything.

MAN: It's the haze out on the sea. It's fogged up our memories.

WOMAN: Fogged, you say? *(He nods)* It was bright earlier. Look how it changes.

MAN: That's the sea for you. *(Pause)* Those two lads . . .,

WOMAN: Yes. Do you know them? The ones swinging on the shelter opposite.

MAN: They seem familiar.

WOMAN: They do?

MAN: It's either the very young or the old who hang out in these places.

WOMAN: Are they brothers?

MAN: I'm not sure.

WOMAN: I like the tall one. I love tall men.

MAN: All tall men?

WOMAN: A good many. I was very disappointed when I found out . . .

MAN: What did you find out?

WOMAN: That one of my favourite actors had to stand on a box when he made his films.

MAN: You must have felt deflated. Mind you, a lot of actors are short-arses.

WOMAN: I cried for a week.

MAN: Was that before or after the brewery?

WOMAN: It could have been concurrent. A week of double disappointment.

MAN: I like the younger one. He's very handsome.

WOMAN: Are you speaking objectively?

MAN: No, not at all. From experience. Look at him swing! He's got a great arse.

WOMAN: It's so refreshing to hear someone so open about their sexuality. It quite turns me on. You're not bad yourself, by the way.

MAN: Good. *(Pause)* But don't look at me!

WOMAN: It's okay. I wasn't. I was looking at my handsome knight swinging.

MAN: What's the other one doing?

WOMAN: He's climbing on the rooftop. He looks like an angel in the sun.

MAN: That roof'll be slippery after the sea fret.

WOMAN: You're-right.

MAN: He'll have difficulty keeping his balance.

WOMAN: If we both run forward, we might be able to catch him; help him.

MAN: Good idea. *(They run towards the shelter)*

SCENE 11

(Ernest approaches the shelter. He looks round for a moment, then sits down.)

ERNEST: That hill was better than what I thought it was going to be. *(Looks out to sea. Takes out some binoculars)* Now, what have we got today? Black-backed gulls, I think. Ah yes, and a fulmar. *(Hilda Jones approaches)* How's the hill, Mrs. Jones?

HILDA: Better, a little better, Mr. H. (Sits down) Quite nice today, isn't it?

ERNEST: I can see you're in a good mood. Yes, not bad at all.

HILDA: And you look pleased with yourself. *(Pause)* You know, somebody told me this morning it was Thursday. I couldn't believe it. I went down to catch the market and they said it was yesterday.

ERNEST: That's very odd, Mrs. Jones, because when the Local Advertiser came through my letter box, I could have sworn it was Thursday.

HILDA: That's a paper I take it.

ERNEST: Of course. What else?

HILDA: So you were expecting Wednesday, too?

ERNEST: Obviously.

HILDA: Those Bank Holidays can play havoc with your indigestion.

ERNEST: But there hasn't been one.

HILDA: True. *(Pause)* That was a lovely evening, wasn't it?

ERNEST: What evening was that?

HILDA: The meal at Eileen's.

ERNEST: Ah yes, indeed. So hospitable. You don't get hospitality like that nowadays.

HILDA: No.

ERNEST: Yes, I'm trying to place when that was. I had an extraordinary feeling that I went to the cinema last night with some youth.

HILDA: I hope you behaved, Mr. H.

ERNEST: No. of course not. I was led astray. But I do remember that dinner and calling you Hilda. I'm so sorry about that.

HILDA: That's quite all right, Mr. H. We was taken out of ourselves.

ERNEST: That's a relief. I wouldn't have wanted you to be upset. You might have cried for a week again.

HILDA: What do you mean for a week again?

ERNEST: You know. When your favourite brewery closed.

HILDA: Who told you about that?

ERNEST: Well, you must have done, Mrs. Jones.

HILDA: I never said anything to you.

ERNEST: How odd. It must have been Eileen, then.

HILDA: I don't remember telling her.

ERNEST: She makes such beautiful cakes. Especially that last one. You know, I can't remember the name.

HILDA: Strange name. Something like, 'we are, we are'. It made no sense. *(Pause)* How's your arthritis, Mr. H?

ERNEST: Better, thanks. A little better.

HILDA: Soon have you up and running, I expect. I was talking to Dolly there last night, or whenever it was. She says she's been going for over 6 months. Says her wonky knee's nearly better.

ERNEST: Well, there's a cause for celebration! A great success. I've always maintained that if you eat the right things. That's why I go to the market.

HILDA: Two journeys, no less. Well, that's good in itself.

ERNEST: Yes.

HILDA: And look at all that stuff they sell in those supermarkets. All chemicals. Sugar and salt.

ERNEST: Bad for you, of course.

HILDA: It is.

ERNEST: And they built over the cricket ground. It makes me so angry.

(The two boys approach the opposite shelter. They sit there and look out)

(Long pause. Both parties watch each other)

HILDA: You know, Mr. H, I have the strangest feeling . . .

ERNEST: It wouldn't be a familiar feeling? Of familiarity?

HILDA: Well, yes. How did you . . . You know, I partly feel that I know those boys. Well, one of them. The good looking one.

ERNEST: Yes.

HILDA: Am I making sense?

ERNEST: As ever, Mrs. Jones. As ever. And I have a strange feeling too that I went to the pictures with the other one.

HILDA: They're not swinging today, not like . . . *(Stops herself)*

ERNEST: They usually do.

HILDA: They seem knackered. Subdued a little.

ERNEST: *(Shivers)* The sun's gone in. I didn't bring a scarf.

HILDA: Let's get up and walk past them. Just to . . .

ERNEST: Yes, let's do that.

HILDA: The older one's getting up. He's slapping the other one on the back.

ERNEST: They seem to be congratulating each other.

HILDA: They're turning.

ERNEST: They're walking away. We'll never catch up with them.

HILDA: We need more of Eileen's cakes if we're going to get anywhere near.

ERNEST: *(Out of breath)* It's no use, Hilda. They've gone. We won't . . .

HILDA: Funny how things change.

ERNEST: Do they?

HILDA: Yes.

ERNEST: It's being by the sea. Coastal weather. Ever changing.

HILDA: The sea is so still.

ERNEST: No birds now. Nothing at all. *(Reaches for his binoculars. Long pause)*

HILDA: Eileen's next dinner party. We've got that to look forward to. We must bring a bottle.

ERNEST: That'll be nice. *(Pause)*

HILDA: The sea is indistinguishable from the sky.

ERNEST: Just a different shade of grey. *(Pause)* No movement. Not that we can see. Nothing . . .

HILDA: Silence.

ERNEST: Not a wave visible.

THE MAKING
OF LUSTRETTA
OR
THE RIGHT POSITION

CAST LIST

Henry—A Composer

Franz—Friend of Henry

Servant

Secretary

Count

Lustretta

Polly—A Maid

Eddie—A Stable Boy

Voice (Offstage)

SCENE 1

(Henry has come to the Winter Palace. He is waiting in one of the rooms. He walks round for a few moments, glances at the table in the centre of the room. Looks round, then walks back to his chair)

HENRY: How much longer is it going to be? I've been here for . . . well over an hour.

VOICE: *(Offstage)* Forty-five minutes.

HENRY: Well, it feels like an hour. And in the circumstances I'm entitled to exaggerate, aren't I?

VOICE: If you say so.

HENRY: I daresay, it's all part of the plan. To keep you waiting. To unsettle you. That way they can bamboozle you into anything.

VOICE: Bamboozle?

HENRY: Yes. You've not heard of that? Well, I can teach you all sorts of words that you won't have heard before. Words that would make your garters curl.

VOICE: I'm not wearing any.

HENRY: It was just an expression, you pedant. *(Walks round again)* Oh, all this waiting!

(The doors open and a servant appears)

SERVANT: If you'd like to step this way, sir. They're ready for you now.

HENRY: They?

SERVANT: Yes.

HENRY: You said *they*. You mean there's more than one?

SERVANT: I'm not sure, sir. There could be.

HENRY: But you said *they*.

SERVANT: Impersonal they. More anonymous, don't you think?

HENRY: And who will *they* be?

SERVANT: Well, the secretary, I should imagine.

HENRY: Not the Count?

SERVANT: No, not the Count. It doesn't usually happen that way.

HENRY: But it's the Count I would be working for?

SERVANT: Yes, sir.

HENRY: Not the secretary?

SERVANT: No, sir.

HENRY: So why do I have to see the secretary?

SERVANT: It's the way it is, sir. The secretary does all the appointments. The hiring and firing. The matching and dispatching.

HENRY: Not the Count, then?

SERVANT: No, sir. Not the Count. You can't count on him. *(Stifles a tee-hee)* Just my little joke, sir.

HENRY: I see. Well, it's hilariously funny.

SERVANT: I would advise haste, sir. The secretary doesn't like to be kept waiting.

(They walk back and across the stage)

HENRY: So many corridors.

SERVANT: It's all due to the size of the building.

HENRY: How do you remember your way?

SERVANT: Before we're taken on, we have to do a kind of test. An orientation thingy. It's called the knowledge.

HENRY: *(Lagging behind)* Oh.

SERVANT: You'll have to keep up, sir. It's most important that we get you there on time. One minute late and he's likely to fly into the most terrible rage.

HENRY: Is that so?

SERVANT: Oh *yes*, sir. *(Turning left)* It's this way now. Follow me.

(They reach the appointed place)

HENRY: I'm quite exhausted with all this walking.

SERVANT: You're obviously not a servant, sir.

HENRY: No.

SERVANT: Would you like to be? I mean, you have that I wonder what it's like to be a servant look.

HENRY: Do I? How extraordinary.

SERVANT: You do. And if you don't mind me saying so, it's not very becoming. We should all know our place.

HENRY: *(Changes facial expression)* There. Is that better?

SERVANT: Much, sir. Now, please wait here.

(Servant leaves. Henry paces up and down the room)

HENRY: What a place! It's huge. How on earth does he manage to find his way about? And imagine living here. It's rattling around like a pea in a drum. I'm not sure I . . .

SECRETARY: *(Enters)* Good day to you, sir.

HENRY: *(Startled)* Ah yes. Yes. Good day indeed.

SECRETARY: You're on your own?

HENRY: Yes.

SECRETARY: Funny. I could have sworn I heard voices.

HENRY: Er, have you seen anyone about that? A doctor, perhaps?

SECRETARY: Very droll. Keep it up and we'll get along famously.

HENRY: I'm sorry. It's just because I'm nervous.

SECRETARY: Nervous? Why? There's no need. Now, let's get down to business.

HENRY: By all means.

SECRETARY: So you're applying for the position of Court Composer?

HENRY: That's right.

SECRETARY: And you know what that entails?

HENRY: Yes. Yes, of course.

SECRETARY: It's not just writing a few tunes. Some merry little ditties.

HENRY: I never thought it was.

SECRETARY: There's the conducting for a start. And then there are rehearsals, of course.

                With the orchestra. Not to mention the commissions.

HENRY: Ah, the commissions. Yes.

SECRETARY: Birthdays, feast days, name days, holidays. You name it.

HENRY: Yes.

SECRETARY: So there it is.

HENRY: I'll be more than happy to.

SECRETARY: The Count can be quite a hard taskmaster.

HENRY: I have no doubt.

SECRETARY: But very fair, sir.

HENRY: Oh yes.

SECRETARY: Now tell me, where did you work before?

HENRY: Has the interview started?

SECRETARY: If you like, yes.

HENRY: Work? Oh yes, er, well. *(To himself)* I don't like questions like this. *(To the Secretary)* I was organist.

SECRETARY: Organist?

HENRY: Yes.

SECRETARY: And where was that?

HENRY: Luderholz-Beckerbrau.

SECRETARY: Luderholz-Beckerbrau? What a beautiful name!

HENRY: Have you heard of it?

SECRETARY: Sadly no.

HENRY: No. Well, not many people have, actually. *(He looks at his watch)*

SECRETARY: Are you expected anywhere?

HENRY: No, no. I was just . . . I often look at it when I get a tune in my head.

SECRETARY: A tune?

HENRY: Yes.

SECRETARY: And do you have one now?

HENRY: The beginnings of one, I think. Yes.

SECRETARY: You have references, I take it?

HENRY: Yes, yes. One moment. *(Fumbles in portable case)* Yes, here
                they are.

SECRETARY: Thank you. *(Reads references)* Yes. *(Pause)* Yes. *(Pause)* Yes.
                (Returns them to Henry)

HENRY: Thank you.

SECRETARY: Well, that all seems to be most satisfactory.

HENRY: I'm glad.

SECRETARY: And in the light of which, I feel we are able to offer you the
                position.

HENRY: You can? You mean? Oh, I'm so . . . I don't know what to say.

                (Rushes round and kisses Secretary on the mouth) Thank you.
                            Thank you so much.

SECRETARY: *(Visibly perturbed)* Steady on there. *(Wipes his mouth with a
                handkerchief)*

HENRY: Oh! Oh! I'm so sorry. I shouldn't. It's just . . . I felt a rush of
                euphoria and . . .

SECRETARY: So I see.

HENRY: It must have been the tune.

SECRETARY: The tune?

HENRY: Yes. And . . . and . . . I've been in Italy. I went there on
                holiday for two weeks. Small village in a wine-growing region.
                Lovely place. Everybody kissed everybody. I am so sorry. I do
                apologise. I just forgot myself. Forgot where I actually was. I
                was so happy when you . . .

SECRETARY: Yes, yes. Well, we'll make no mention of that.

HENRY: No, no. So, er, when do I start?

SECRETARY: The first of next month.

HENRY: I see. And is the previous incumbent still here? My predecessor?

SECRETARY: He left last week.

HENRY: So suddenly?

SECRETARY: You *could* say.

HENRY: May I ask what happened?

SECRETARY: *(Cautiously)* Well, I suppose you'll get to know sooner or later, tittle-tattle being what it is.

HENRY: Tittle-tattle?

SECRETARY: He ran off with one of the servants.

HENRY: Most remiss.

SECRETARY: Said they were both in love.

HENRY: Ah well.

SECRETARY: The Count was furious.

HENRY: I can imagine.

SECRETARY: Said Micky was his best gardener.

HENRY: Micky?

SECRETARY: It turns out *all* the compositions were dedicated to him. 'As I walk through a field of watermelons,' 'When thrushes tiptoe across the lawn'. It was a devastating body-blow, I can tell you.

HENRY: Nothing stays fixed, I suppose. Everything can wobble from precarious foundations.

SECRETARY: Pardon? Oh yes, I see. Well don't *you* go getting any ideas!

HENRY: Of course not. The gardening retinue will be quite safe with me. I only have eyes for the ladies.

SECRETARY: That's what Giuseppe said.

HENRY: It's a promise I intend to keep.

SCENE 2

(Village inn. Henry and Franz)

HENRY: I was completely taken aback, I can tell you. I mean, I never thought I'd get the job.

FRANZ: Well there you are. It often happens when you lower your expectations.

HENRY: Once I got there, saw how big the place was, the spacious gardens and the grounds, I thought, Henry, my boy, you're possibly way out of your depth.

FRANZ: Did they have any other applicants?

HENRY: Not that I know of. Well, I didn't see any.

FRANZ: It's your lucky day, then.

HENRY: I nearly thought I'd blown it.

FRANZ: Blown it?

HENRY: When he offered me the job, I got up and kissed him.

FRANZ: I thought that happened once you started working.

HENRY: I was so overwhelmed. I think he's forgotten it.

FRANZ: Probably traumatised for life, poor fellow.

HENRY: That's a little harsh. Now, come, let us drink to my amazing fortune. Landlord, the same again, please.

SCENE 3

(Baroque music. Slow dance across the stage. Henry arrives at the Winter Palace with a suitcase. He stands outside watching.)

HENRY: I could have sworn it's got bigger since I was last here.

VOICE: That's because you have time to take it in. Last time you were concentrating on your act.

HENRY: It was no act. You know that. And I *did* play the organ a few times.

VOICE: Twice, if I recall.

HENRY: The organist had been stung by a wasp. His fingers swelled up.

VOICE: Two services, that's all.

HENRY: I learnt much from the experience.

VOICE: You're going to have to carry this off, you know.

HENRY: I do wish you'd be quiet.

SERVANT: *(Opens door)* Welcome to you, sir.

HENRY: Er, yes. Thank you. I didn't ring.

SERVANT: No. I was waiting behind the door all morning.

HENRY: You were? Oh, were you? Oh, I see now. You're joking.

SERVANT: You know me. But actually, I heard voices.

HENRY: Voices? Oh, I see.

SERVANT: I heard voices outside, so naturally I came towards the door.

HENRY: Ah yes. I was rehearsing, you see.

SERVANT: I seemed to hear *two* voices.

HENRY: That's because I do *both* parts.

SERVANT: It's most versatile, sir. I'm sure you'll be an asset to us all. Follow me.

(They walk through numerous corridors) I'll take you to your room now.

HENRY: Thank you. *(Pause)* I expect I'll need a ball of string with me for the first week.

SERVANT: String? You need string? I'll ask cook if she has any.

HENRY: It was a jest, actually.

SERVANT: A joke?

HENRY: You see, you don't have the monopoly.

SERVANT: But why would you need string, sir? Unless it's a problem with the piano.

HENRY: Piano? Ah, very good. Do you know what kind it is?

SERVANT: A fortepiano, sir.

HENRY: I see. And what exactly is wrong with it?

SERVANT: Nothing, sir. It works perfectly.

HENRY: But I thought . . .

SERVANT: A fortepiano, sir. They're the latest rage. It's goodbye to harpsichords now.

HENRY: *(Nonchalantly)* I suppose it must be.

SCENE 4

(Servant shows Henry the room)

SERVANT: This is your room, sir.

HENRY: There's a good view onto the garden. *(Walks around)* It's a bit small, though.

SERVANT: The musicians always have this room, sir. It's a tradition.

HENRY: Well we wouldn't want to discontinue that. Upset the applecart.

SERVANT: Is there anything else I can get you?

HENRY: *(Looking out of the window)* No, no. That's fine. *(Pause)* Tell me, there's a woman walking towards the shrubbery. Who is that?

SERVANT: I can't see anyone, sir.

HENRY: To your right, man.

SERVANT: I need my glasses. I'm a little short-sighted.

HENRY: She looks a pretty thing.

SERVANT: Well, sir, without my glasses and not having seen the lady in question, I'd hazard a guess that it could be the Lady Lustretta.

HENRY: Lustretta? What an unusual name! Look, there she goes again.

SERVANT: I'm hopeless without my glasses, sir.

HENRY: And yet you navigated me here without mishap or hiccup.

SERVANT: That's different, sir. A sort of homing instinct.

HENRY: You know, I could have sworn this place has become bigger since last time.

SERVANT: I wouldn't let the Count hear you say that, sir.

HENRY: Hear me what?

SERVANT: Calling his Winter Palace a place.

HENRY: But it seems, with the exception of this room, of course, to have expanded since my last visit.

SERVANT: I daresay, sir. Anyway, I'm sure you'll find your way around.

HENRY: Yes, I'm sure I will too.

SERVANT: Will that be all, sir?

HENRY: For the time being.

SERVANT: Very good. *(Servant leaves)*

VOICE: *(Offstage, with an American accent)*

And . . . and . . . I want to just say . . . oh my . . . I guess . . . well . . . I want to say . . . I never thought to get an honour like this and it means so much to me . . . because . . . of all the work . . . and I want to . . . well . . . give my thanks to all . . . especially my family *(chokes back a sob)* and most of all . . . to my goldfish . . . because . . . you know *(Weeps)* he's always . . . been there for me . . . and I am so nervous . . . and honoured to receive this truly wonderful award. So thank you, Oscar . . .

(Ripples of applause)

SCENE 5

(Henry is walking in the shrubbery. Lady Lustretta gives a start)

LUSTRETTA: Sir, you startled me.

HENRY: I am so sorry. It was not my intention. Permit me to introduce myself.

LUSTRETTA: Are you alone?

HENRY: It would appear so.

LUSTRETTA: Strange. I thought I could hear voices.

HENRY: It must be the wind blowing through the trees.

LUSTRETTA: I distinctly heard a voice. A strange voice. And someone calling Oscar.

HENRY: That'll be the dog, I expect.

LUSTRETTA: There is no dog, as far as I know.

HENRY: A visiting dog, then.

LUSTRETTA: Do dogs visit?

HENRY: Or perhaps the cat?

LUSTRETTA: It seems a funny name for a cat. We used to have one once.

HENRY: Idle beasts. They just lie around all day. Not unlike the aristocracy.

LUSTRETTA: Mercy, sir. Do you mean the Count?

HENRY: I was alluding to no one, madam. I was speaking metaphorically and symbolically.

LUSTRETTA: Were you? *(Pause)* Oh look! There's a stain on your trousers.

HENRY: Is there? How remiss of me!

LUSTRETTA: I have a handkerchief.

HENRY: That's most kind.

LUSTRETTA: You must have brushed against something on your way to the garden.

HENRY: It's to be expected, I suppose.

LUSTRETTA: It's a bit like sloe.

HENRY: Pardon?

LUSTRETTA: Either that or elder.

HENRY: Elder, I know. But sloe?

LUSTRETTA: You wouldn't want to eat one. It makes your mouth dry up. Oooh, it's so bitter. I'm going to have to rub it a bit harder.

HENRY: Whatever you feel, my dear lady. I'm at your disposal.

LUSTRETTA: Oh no, I wouldn't want to dispose of you. We've only just met.

HENRY: This is true. And I'm enjoying the experience very much.

LUSTRETTA: I'm *so* glad.

HENRY: Why's that?

LUSTRETTA: Because it's Monday.

HENRY: I see. And, by the way, are you Lustretta?

LUSTRETTA: I am, sir. Who told you that?

HENRY: I saw you from the window. The servant pointed you out, although he didn't have his glasses.

LUSTRETTA: He did? And you *are*?

HENRY: I wasn't permitted to introduce myself.

LUSTRETTA: When was that?

HENRY: Earlier I said to you 'Permit me to introduce myself' and it went unheeded.

LUSTRETTA: How careless of me. Besides, I'm hopeless with names.

HENRY: But you have such a beautiful name.

LUSTRETTA: Do you think so?

HENRY: I do.

LUSTRETTA: I don't like Hermione much.

HENRY: Hermione? But I thought it was Lustretta?

LUSTRETTA: Lustretta. Oh yes, that's right. I did say I was hopeless with names. The Count's nephew Jonathan tried to teach me.

HENRY: Is he here now?

LUSTRETTA: He's away on business. He said he would spank me each time I forgot.

HENRY: The brute! And did he?

LUSTRETTA: Oh yes! Very much so. In fact I enjoyed it so much I made no effort to remember at all. You could say it's made a lasting impression on me.

HENRY: The scoundrel!

LUSTRETTA: Which is why I forget names now, sir. Sort of ingrained.

HENRY: It's a disgraceful state of affairs. How old was the nephew?

LUSTRETTA: Twenty two.

HENRY: Oh well, that's all right, then.

LUSTRETTA: He said he was doing it for my benefit.

HENRY: I'm sure he was. Anyway, my name is . . .

LUSTRETTA: No, don't confuse me, sir. I have enough on my plate. It takes me all my time to remember that I'm not Hermione.

HENRY: Very well, then. I won't. And do you have another name? A family name?

LUSTRETTA: I'm trying to remember it. Yes. Yes. Now I've got it. A . . . M . . . O . . . er, yes there's an R . . . and an E.

HENRY: Amore. That spells Amore. How beautiful!

LUSTRETTA: It is when *you* say it. They all call me Amery or Emery. Emery makes me really cross.

HENRY: Lustretta Amore. It's most beautiful. It's like a starlit evening with just the hint of moon. No wind.

LUSTRETTA: Is it after dinner, sir?

HENRY: Why yes, it would be.

LUSTRETTA: Then there'll be plenty.

HENRY: I don't see the connection.

LUSTRETTA: The wind always starts at 9 o'clock. Just after the cabbage soup. It's as regular as clockwork. Quite awful, in fact.

HENRY: There is a hint of lavender as your cloak brushes past, and beyond the arch a scent of honeysuckle luring out the night moths.

LUSTRETTA: I'm very annoyed with them. They chewed my shawl to ribbons.

HENRY: Ah now, if you put lavender in your drawers.

LUSTRETTA: *(Gasps)* You are *most* impertinent, sir.

HENRY: Where you keep them.

LUSTRETTA: Pardon?

HENRY: Where you keep them.

LUSTRETTA: Why do you want to know where I keep them?

HENRY: I don't.

LUSTRETTA: You did.

HENRY: I didn't.

LUSTRETTA: You said where you keep them.

HENRY: It was not a question.

LUSTRETTA: It wasn't?

HENRY: No.

LUSTRETTA: Oh, I'm so sorry, then.

HENRY: I was meaning moths wouldn't like the lavender. Or wormwood for that matter.

LUSTRETTA: There's none of that in my bedroom, though they did have some in the library once. Little tiny holes. Musty smell.

HENRY: I mean wormwood, the plant. Not what you're thinking of.

LUSTRETTA: Oh I see. *(Pause)* I'm so sorry. What must you think of me? I've made a fool of myself. I must rub a little harder to get the stain out. *(She rubs)* Yes. There we are.

HENRY: *(Gasps)* Oh yes. Yes, you must! You must!

SCENE 6

(Henry in the salon by the piano)

HENRY: I wish I had one of these in my bedroom. I feel so exposed here, tinkering away.

VOICE: Not as exposed as you were in the shrubbery. And on *first* acquaintance!

HENRY: *She* volunteered!

VOICE: You rose to the occasion magnificently.

HENRY: I was thinking about her name. You know, how I could improve on it.

VOICE: Improve on perfection?

HENRY: Who said anything about perfection?

VOICE: Well, you did, in the shrubbery. You shouted it out. The lady ran away. I'm sure they must have heard you up at the house.

HENRY: It was not my intention to be so . . .

VOICE: Naughty?

HENRY: Noisy. *(Pause)* Perhaps I should go and see the nephew.

VOICE: Now you've lost me.

HENRY: I wish I could. *(Pause)* Well, there's work to do and composing to be done.

(Plays a few bars)

VOICE: *That's* what you call it!

HENRY: *(Angrily)* Who asked you? *(Crosses out on the score)* Right. Try
              again.

              (Plays again. Crosses out) This composing lark is more difficult
              than I thought. Nobody told me about that.

SCENE 7

(Enter the Count, looking not unlike the Secretary. Fanfare)

COUNT: Good morning, Henry. *(Henry gets up)* Now don't get up. I like to see a man hard at it, which is obviously what you're doing. *(Motions to him to sit down)* No, no.

I insist. I'm just looking for a book. I left it behind last night. We had a bit of a soiree in here. I'm always leaving things behind. *(Laughs)* Still, it'll turn up, I'm sure. Yes, jolly good. Carry on. *(Laughs and leaves)*

HENRY: Well I'll be . . . That's the first time I've met him. What a man! What an honour! And so virile! Not like that sallow secretary. There's something unpleasant about him. Creepy. As if you never know what he's thinking. But the Count . . . Well, I'm full of admiration for him already. Straight as a die. It's an honour to work for him. *(Plays a more vigorous tune)* A little better.

VOICE: Yes, a little better.

HENRY: I thought you'd gone.

VOICE: You'll be there in time.

HENRY: You think so?

VOICE: Give it another thirty years, perhaps. *(Henry throws the manuscript in anger)*

SCENE 8

(Polly, a maid and Eddie, a stable-boy)

POLLY: I've got my work cut out today.

EDDIE: Why's that, Polly?

POLLY: It's that Mister Henry.

EDDIE: Mister Henry the musician?

POLLY: The very same. He was out again last night. Down the Frog and Parrot.

EDDIE: A man's entitled to a little entertainment . . . and some refreshment.

POLLY: I'm not arguing with that. No, it's just he used up half a year's refreshment all at once.

EDDIE: Was he tipsy?

POLLY: Paralytic. Kept saying I'm Brahms and . . . that other person.

EDDIE: Then what did he do?

POLLY: He opened the piano and . . .

EDDIE: Ugh! Disgusting!

POLLY: *(Angrily)* Yes. And muggins here has to clean it up. Render it serviceable, Mrs. Bridges said.

EDDIE: Did she? Does the Secretary know?

POLLY: Not likely. He'd have a fit.

EDDIE: And the Count?

POLLY: He was sozzled himself last night.

EDDIE: Was he indeed?

POLLY: Pissed as a proverbial. He has no recollection.

EDDIE: What a bunch!

POLLY: You *could* say that.

EDDIE: *(Pause)* Come, Polly, I think you need some consolation. *(Goes to grab her)*

POLLY: *(Pushes him away)* Not now, Ed. I've got too much to do.

EDDIE: I'm only trying to help.

POLLY: Yes, I know you are. *(Goes over towards the piano)*

EDDIE: What are you doing now?

POLLY: I'm rubbing lavender oil on the piano.

EDDIE: Does that improve the sound?

POLLY: No, but it'll take away . . .

EDDIE: I see what you mean. What a stink!

POLLY: The good thing is I'm sure he'll be a little sheepish for a few days. Guilty, you know. And he'll be on his best behaviour.

EDDIE: Like me, you mean. *(Goes to grab her)*

SCENE 9

(Henry and Polly in the study. Henry is at the piano)

POLLY: Good morning, Mister Henry.

HENRY: *(Rubs his head)* Hello.

POLLY: *(Starts cleaning. After a few moments, she looks at Henry)* Are
            you all right, Mister Henry?

HENRY: I'm just a little tired, that's all.

POLLY: Sorry to hear that, Mister Henry.

HENRY: Nothing that a drink won't fix, of course. *(He pulls out a brandy
            bottle)*

POLLY: *(Stops him)*

HENRY: Polly, what are you doing? Have you taken leave of your
            senses?

POLLY: I don't think that's a good idea, sir.

HENRY: And why ever not?

POLLY: You were singing last night.

HENRY: I was?

POLLY: Yes, sir. Loudly.

HENRY: That's funny. I have no recollection. What was I singing?

POLLY: A new Cantata for the library, sir. Only it seemed a bit rude.

HENRY: Cantata? But I've never written a Cantata.

POLLY: Well you did last night.

HENRY: And how did it sound?

POLLY: Like nothing I've heard before.

HENRY: Really? I see. Well I appear to have broken new ground, then. Perhaps I should visit the Frog more often.

POLLY: The frog, sir?

HENRY: The Frog and Parrot. Or whatever it's called.

POLLY: I don't think that's a good idea, sir.

HENRY: Why's that, Polly?

POLLY: Well, apart from the obvious damage to windows, it sounded like the frog singing, you see.

HENRY: Really? Well, I *am* a baritone.

POLLY: Or it could have been the parrot. The problems all started when you tried to do all the different voices.

HENRY: Voices?

POLLY: Yes, sir.

HENRY: Well I shall take your advice to heart.

POLLY: Thank you. *(Pause)* Would you like some tea, sir?

HENRY: No, I'm all right, Polly. I think I'll give my stomach a rest for a while.

POLLY: It's probably best, sir.

HENRY: It's heartening to have your encouragement. *(Opens piano. Closes it immediately)* On second thoughts, I think it's too early to practise. *(Sniffs)*

POLLY: Is everything all right, sir?

HENRY: Yes, I think so. Hmm! There's a very strange smell in this room, Polly. Do you know anything about it?

SCENE 10

(Henry is practising when the Count enters)

COUNT: Ah, good morning to you, sir.

HENRY: Good morning, Your Grace.

COUNT: Pardon?

HENRY: Your Grace.

COUNT: No, I'm not, sir. I'm the Count. Have you forgotten?

HENRY: Oh. No, sir.

COUNT: Good. And how are we today?

HENRY: Just a little weary, sir.

COUNT: You must be overdoing it. Burning the midnight oil.

HENRY: That'll be it, Your . . .

COUNT: One of the servants said you were serenading them in the library last night.

HENRY: Oh well, I do apologise. I forgot the hour.

COUNT: No need to, my dear fellow. Devotion to duty. It's admirable in a man.

HENRY: Thank you, sir.

COUNT: *(Sniffs)* I must say, there's a damned odd smell in here.

HENRY: Is there, sir?

COUNT: Yes. Let me open a window. *(Sniffs again)* It seems to be coming from the piano.

HENRY: Is it?

COUNT: Yes.

HENRY: Perhaps it's begging for attention.

COUNT: Sort of apricot smell.

HENRY: Indeed.

COUNT: It'll be the ladies, I expect. You can't trust them, you know. Any excuse.

HENRY: No, sir. *(Count leaves the room quickly)*

HENRY: *(To audience)* I sat in that freezing room all day. I declined food. I know a man has to suffer for his art but it was the stomach that held sway. And not a tune would surface. Nothing. Not even a ditty. I tried one thing and then another. And when something did come along, I realised it was a tune one of the servants had been humming all day. *(Gets up, walks around. Sits down)* Perhaps I should come clean and hand in my notice.

          (Gets up again) But it's *such* a beautiful place. It's a delight to be here. The air in the morning when you fling open the windows. The vast stretch of grassland leading up to the woods. The herb garden and the scented shrubbery. Ah, the shrubbery. And then there's the sound of silence, of stillness, broken only by the rows of whispering trees behind the house.

VOICE: Such poetry!

HENRY: Pardon?

VOICE:	You heard. I said such poetry.
HENRY:	Is a man entitled to no privacy?
VOICE:	We seem a little sensitive today.
HENRY:	Is it any wonder? Anyway, if you've come here to mock.
VOICE:	I was merely commenting.
HENRY:	It's music I'm here for, not poetry, in case that's escaped your notice.
VOICE:	It hasn't.
HENRY:	And I can't write a bloody note.
VOICE:	There speaks the voice of a self-indulgent hangover.
HENRY:	And tomorrow I'll be sober.
VOICE:	Yes.
HENRY:	And there'll be no difference.
VOICE:	I didn't like to say but as you've put it . . . *(Pause)* Then you shouldn't have . . .
HENRY:	Yes, yes. I know. But when I saw the house lying beyond the gates, I was tempted. A new life. And I felt a little . . . a need for . . .
VOICE:	Social climbing?
HENRY:	If you like, yes. And why not? Why *not* attempt the impossible?
VOICE:	Difficult for men.
HENRY:	For men?
VOICE:	Yes.
HENRY:	You think so?
VOICE:	I know so.

HENRY: How do you know?

VOICE: Trust me. I do. How near the sun flew mighty Icarus, so that his wings were swiftly singed . . . and all of a sudden . . .

HENRY: You've lost me.

VOICE: It's not difficult.

HENRY: If you've got nothing sensible to say, other than come out with these obscure ramblings . . . and about people I've never heard of . . . then . . .

VOICE: Then?

HENRY: You might as well go.

VOICE: That's a little harsh, not to say tetchy.

HENRY: I don't need anyone. Least of all *you*!

VOICE: Oh I think you do.

HENRY: No one.

VOICE: Think back. Think back to your main achievement here.

HENRY: What achievement?

VOICE: As if you need reminding.

HENRY: I'm ashamed to.

VOICE: Never turn away a helping hand.

HENRY: That's what I say to myself each morning.

VOICE: I'm not talking about that.

HENRY: You're not?

VOICE: No. Listen to me for a moment. Come off your pedestal and look around you.

HENRY: Look around me? What do you mean?

VOICE: I've gone.

HENRY: No you haven't.

VOICE: You told me to go.

HENRY: No, I didn't. Come back. *(Silence)* I didn't. I didn't.

(Characters move across the stage in masks. Music.)

SCENE 11

(Henry alone. There is a knocking at his door, which he does not hear. Knocking continues. Lustretta enters. Henry looks startled.)

LUSTRETTA: I did knock, sir. I can assure you.

HENRY: Did you? I didn't hear.

LUSTRETTA: Perhaps I should have knocked louder but I didn't want to disturb you.

HENRY: Don't worry. There's nothing to disturb.

LUSTRETTA: How so, sir? I feel there *must* be. Genius at work and all that.

HENRY: Hardly genius. *(Pause)*

LUSTRETTA: You seem a little low in spirit.

HENRY: Yes, so low I'm grovelling.

LUSTRETTA: Pardon? I don't understand.

HENRY: No matter.

LUSTRETTA: Is there *anything* I can do?

HENRY: I want to be alone.

LUSTRETTA: Do you really? How appalling!

HENRY: *(Looks at her)* Yes.

LUSTRETTA: Are you sure?

HENRY: *(Looks again)* No, not anymore. Come here, my sweet. Oh, how I adore your tiny feet.

LUSTRETTA: Oh my! *(They embrace)* Ever since I saw you in the shrubbery, I knew, I thought, this is the man.

HENRY: And I . . . was overcome by your radiance. The sun shone all day.

LUSTRETTA: It's nice of you to say.

HENRY: Come closer, my sweet! My angel!

LUSTRETTA: Sir, you are most naughty again.

HENRY: *(Growls)* You ain't seen nothing yet!

LUSTRETTA: Pardon, sir?

HENRY: Come here, you naughty thing, you infinite tease.

(They disrobe a little. There is a clunk from the piano as they do this)

LUSTRETTA: Oh, sir.

HENRY: Sweet endless temptation!

LUSTRETTA: Sir!

HENRY: I shall name you Miss d'Amore. That is what you need . . . in front of your name. And no one shall ever call you Emery again. What an insult! You shall be . . . Miss Lustretta . . . Lustretta d'Amore. *(Sound of guitar music)*

LUSTRETTA: If you say so, sir.

HENRY: I do. You shall be *my* Lustretta!

LUSTRETTA: Yes.

HENRY: I feel the air is heady, intoxicating.

LUSTRETTA: That could be because you're still drunk, sir.

HENRY: Nonsense! Nonsense! Poppycock! I am intoxicated and overwhelmed by you. My angel of the shrubbery!

LUSTRETTA: What if someone should come in?

HENRY: Then I should lock the door.

LUSTRETTA: And we would be alone together.

HENRY: Precisely so. *(Pause)* We would.

VOICE: Not quite.

HENRY: Shut up, you idiot! Not now!

LUSTRETTA: *(Alarmed)* Pardon, sir? Why do you shout?

HENRY: Shout? I wasn't shouting.

LUSTRETTA: Yes you were. You said shut up.

HENRY: I did?

LUSTRETTA: I distinctly heard you. And you said you idiot.

HENRY: That'll be them in the kitchen. They're always rowing.

LUSTRETTA: Are they?

HENRY: They are. And if I was shouting, I was shouting for joy. Come let us not apply too much rationale. I don't want our romantic moment to be spoilt.

LUSTRETTA: I couldn't hear them, sir. Nor the owls.

HENRY: No, you wouldn't. Only a musician would. Only someone with finely tuned and sensitive hearing *(She turns to face him)* The owls?

LUSTRETTA: They are nice ears, aren't they?

HENRY: If you say so, my sweet. Oh I am consumed in a cloud of lust. Come nearer to the piano stool. Yes, that's it.

(As Lustretta moves up and down on Henry's knee a beautiful tune is heard from the piano)

LUSTRETTA: That's so clever of you, sir.

HENRY: Clever of me? What is?

LUSTRETTA: Well, sir, to play, a melody whilst on the job.

HENRY: But my hands are nowhere near the piano. *(He grabs her tightly)*

LUSTRETTA: Ooh! So they aren't.

HENRY: Nowhere near.

LUSTRETTA: No.

HENRY: *(Puzzled)* So how come the music is playing and sounding so sweetly?

LUSTRETTA: No idea. But it must be *something* you're doing.

HENRY: Perhaps, Lustretta.

LUSTRETTA: Henry?

HENRY: I love it when you call me Henry. Maybe . . .

LUSTRETTA: Yes.

HENRY: Maybe, it is just the music of love.

LUSTRETTA: You think so? Well, it is beautiful whatever it is.

HENRY: *(To audience)* The melodies flowed for a good half hour and in the meantime the piano stool stood up nobly. It endured the extra impact with fortitude and was bravely borne. But where was the music coming from? For, in truth, neither of us had their hands on the piano. Such melodies! Such harmonies and inventions! And then it gradually began to dawn on me and the revelation was as amazing as it was perplexing. The same melodies were coming forth as a result of the lovely Lady Lustretta's pert posterior brushing up and down against the keyboard. I couldn't believe it and nor could she! For as she bounced up and down, swaying back and forth onto me, she was wholly and blissfully unaware! It was a musical behind of the greatest magnitude, and I was playing it, exposing its charms to all the world in a truly sensational debut. I am sure the tunes from the piano drew favourable comments from the footsteps that passed up and down the corridor, and they may even have stopped to listen. There were oohs and aahs, and ejaculations of admiration, but then I realised some of them were in fact myself, for in that room of tender intimacy, the sounds reverberated off the walls and pinged off the china plates suspended there. But truly, some came from outside and I even thought to have caught a little applause, were it not for an errant foot kicking away a music stand. It was fantastic, marvellous! Quite stupendous. Then eventually all became quiet again. Lustretta tiptoed softly away; the music from those wonderful cheeks had ceased, and I lay languishing, half-asleep, on my music stool.

(Lute music)

HENRY: After that momentous visit and totally unexpected outcome, I wrote down all the tunes I could remember.

VOICE: It took you several goes.

HENRY: As if I needed reminding. *(Pause)* Then I began to think I needed a secretary. The music was coming thick and fast. Outside the door, we hung a sign as the Lady Lustretta came to visit me and together we performed our duets. We practised different tempi and unusual rhythms. I'm all for experimentation, she had said. The critic de Melbray pointed out some while after that there were some unusual syncopations to the fore. 'All in a day's work', I replied. De Melbray remarked on the modesty of the composer. 'It is nothing', I said, 'but forgive me, gentlemen, but I must get back to the drawing board',where in fact Lustretta was waiting eagerly for my return. I clasped her to me and in our customary adopted positions, we made our beautiful music together. Hark!

EPILOGUE

Ladies and gentlemen,
The censor of the day,
Well, he must have his way.
His views shall naturally hold sway.
And we must, of course, obey.

No other bottom could give such charms,
Not Polly, not Eddie, nor even the composer's arse.
His job was now secure.
The lady ever modest and demure
In her demeanour.

Let us now set aside our rhyme and reason.
New meaning is given to the well-worn saying
'Behind every successful man there lies a woman.'
And, in this case, in front is also true.

For Henry, no man is happier than he.
The Count, of course, excited too.
With Lustretta, so blissfully unaware,
In ignorance of her beautous asset.
So let us salute them both,
For, as we speak,

(Piano tinkling and arpeggios are heard)

They are working on their latest opus.

Hark!

(Music continues and fades)

NIGHT MUSIC

CAST LIST

Ivanovich

Boris—A Servant

Ekaterina Kutlikova—A Pianist

(Centre stage. A wooden chair and table. Behind the table is a full length mirror. There is a phone on the table.
A man enters. He is dressed in a heavy overcoat. He walks up to the mirror, admires the overcoat for a moment, then sits down. Silence. The phone rings. He picks it up)

IVANOVICH: Yes. Speaking. Oh, it's you. *(Laughs. Leans back in the chair)*

(Enter waiter/servant who brings drink on a tray. Ivanovich leans forward to take a sip)

So what can I do for you? Don't tell me this is a social call, otherwise I'll alert the servants I've just seen a flying pig.

(Laughs)

It isn't. Good. How am I? Fine. Fine. I've just got myself a new overcoat. Very nice. You know what our winters are like.

(Takes another sip)

Some assistance? How much? A lot of assistance. I see. Yes, yes.

(*Silence*)

No, I agree. But there has to be a price. Oh yes. After all, we're not a charity. What's that you say? I'm sounding like a capitalist. Did I ever say I wasn't one? I'll send you a box of cigars along with my latest joke. Would you like to hear it? It goes like this. Capitalism is the exploitation of one man by another. And Communism . . . well, it's the other way round.

(*Guffaws*)

Yes, I thought you would like it. So, yes, back to business. Our price, our reward. Our little carrot. 50/50. So, of course, when it's all over, we'll want our little share. How about we take a pen and divide up the map? That's right. A little cushion round our girth. Can you blame us? Look at history. Everybody has tried to do it to us. Everybody. Even you. Well it's time to pick ourselves up. The beaten donkey deserves a carrot.

(*Pause*)

Take it or leave it, my friend. The way things are going, I don't think you're really in a position to bargain. Your little friend across the pond doesn't seem willing to help you. They'll be there in the last few minutes to make films. You'll see. You see I think they rather like that little upstart, that failed painter. Bolshy basher, I think they call him.

(*Pause*)

Just go away and think about it. I can smell your cigar from this end of the telephone. Either that or you're drunk again.

(*Another sip. Puts the phone down. Walks to the mirror*)

A capital coat! Yes, I feel lucky tonight.

Year 1953.

(*A table is laid for four people. Servants busy around the table.*

Ivanovich enters, more slowly this time. He looks tired. Sits down on a chair slightly at an angle to the table)

IVANOVICH: Boris! Boris! Who have I invited tonight?

BORIS: Why sir, don't you remember?

IVANOVICH: If I did I wouldn't be asking you.

(*Boris comes closer, whispers in his ear*)

IVANOVICH: I see, I see. The usual rabble. Nothing changes.

BORIS: But sir, *you* invited them.

IVANOVICH: Of course I invited them, but it's so *boring* seeing the same old faces.

BORIS: *(Slightly worried)* But sir, will we be expecting some *new* faces
                soon?

IVANOVICH: *(Sighs)* No, no. Don't you worry! I've had enough of that for
                the time being.

                (Music can be heard from the kitchen. Ivanovich growls)

                Don't they ever turn their music down? I suppose they think
                I'm getting deaf, but I can tell you, I *still* hear everything.

                (Boris has turned rather pale)

BORIS: Really, sir? *(Apologetically)* I'll ask them to turn it down. I don't
                think they realised they were disturbing you.

IVANOVICH: *(Appears not to have heard Boris. Follows the music with head
                movements)* Hmm! I like that. What is it?

BORIS: I'll find out for you, sir.

IVANOVICH: *(Glances at the newspaper.)* I see my friend, the Englishman got
                back in power.

BORIS: That's an old newspaper, sir.

IVANOVICH: It's an old Englishman, Boris. *(Pause)* But they brought *him*
                back. *(Laughs)*

BORIS: Yes, sir.

IVANOVICH: Who'd have thought it? Bounced back like a snowball on a
                roof. Just when we thought he'd had it, he's back for more.

BORIS: You should never underestimate the stupidity of the electorate,
                sir.

IVANOVICH: Ha! Electorate! And what would you know about that?

BORIS: I think they got tired of Socialism, sir.

IVANOVICH: You call that Socialism! More like a bunch of Methodists than Marxists.

BORIS: Yes, sir. *(Pause)*

IVANOVICH: I wanted to be a priest once, you know. And look at me now. Maybe I should have.

BORIS: *(Pretends to be shocked)* You, sir?

IVANOVICH: Don't pretend you didn't know. Oh, I expect they all have a good laugh about it behind my back. When they're in the kitchen washing up.

BORIS: *(Alarmed)* No, sir!

IVANOVICH: I'd have given them some sermons, I can tell you! Oh yes! Instead of all this cold-war hot air . . . Still, I got what I wanted. Look at the map now! A little protection from our bloody neighbours. And when the time is right *(Music gets louder)*

BORIS: *(Remembering)* I'll go and find out, sir.

IVANOVICH: Find out what?

BORIS: The music.

IVANOVICH: Oh yes, of course. Run along, there's a good fellow! And be quick about it.

(Sits for a moment. Head droops.)

BORIS: *(Returns with a drink)* A piano concerto, sir.

IVANOVICH: *(Gazes in mock astonishment)* A piano concerto. I'd never have guessed. Which one? Whose?

BORIS: *(Flees from the stage. Returns in a minute, during which Ivanovich gazes at the audience)* Mozart, sir. Number 23. Do you need the Koechel number?

IVANOVICH: That won't be necessary.

BORIS: It's a live recording.

IVANOVICH: *(Leans back and listens)* It's beautiful. *(Suddenly sits up.)* I want the record!

BORIS: Pardon, sir?

IVANOVICH: If it's a recording, I want the record. A record made. Want it here. Listen to it here in the comfort of my own room. I don't want some idiot bodyguard sniffing all through the performance. And the coughing! The Englishman said they eat sweets in their concert halls, popcorn in the cinemas.

BORIS: Popcorn?

IVANOVICH: You wouldn't understand, you buffoon! *(Pause)* I want the record here tomorrow morning. Is that understood?

BORIS*:*   *(Anxiously)* Yes, sir. *(Leaves stage wringing hands)*

(Ivanovich sleeps)

(Two hours later)

BORIS: Sir?

IVANOVICH: *(Wakes slowly)* What time is it?

BORIS: Late, sir. Late.

IVANOVICH: How late is late?

BORIS: After eleven. They've been contacted but, er, I'm afraid the pianist, Ekaterina or Doonyasha, or whatever her name is, is being difficult.

IVANOVICH: *(Roars) Difficult? Difficult?*

BORIS: Says she's tired, sir.

IVANOVICH: Tired? Well, *I'm* tired. Have been for years. It's a funny state of affairs when the most powerful chap in the world can't get some piano woman to play a note for him. *(Stretches out a hand)* Phone!

BORIS: *(Trembles. Passes phone. Drops it. Picks it up hurriedly)* Here you are, sir.

IVANOVICH: *(Sighs. Dials. Slams down the phone)* Engaged! Engaged*! (Dials again, this time more impatiently)* At last! *(Pause)* Yes, who's that? *(Angrily)* Is it? Well, I don't want *you!* Get me the bloody pianist! *(Waits)* Difficult! Difficult!

BORIS: *(Waits anxiously)*

IVANOVICH: *(Screams)* What! What! Says she's busy!

BORIS: *(Drops a glass. Fumbles around)* I'm so sorry.

IVANOVICH: *(Looks up at Boris suddenly)* What do you think of Mozart?

BORIS: Mozart?

IVANOVICH: Yes. He's a genius, isn't he?

BORIS: *(Puzzled)* Yes, well he does write some nice tunes, sir, but personally I prefer some of our . . . you know . . . Always thought it's a pity he's not Russian.

IVANOVICH: Poppycock! Is he or is he *not* a genius?

BORIS: A genius, sir. Yes. Undoubtedly.

IVANOVICH: *(Sarcastically)* Thank you. *(Points to the receiver.)* They're trying to get her to come to the phone.

BORIS: *(Aside)* The woman must be crazy. Does she know whom she's talking to?

IVANOVICH: *(Points again to the phone. Smiles)* She's coming.

(For the phone call EKATERINA KUTLIKOVA appears on stage)

EKATERINA: Well, what do you want?

IVANOVICH: Greetings, comrade, how . . .

EKATERINA: Don't give me that shit! What do you *want?* Can't you see I'm busy?

IVANOVICH: *(To Boris. Surprised)* Does she *always* talk like this?

BORIS: *(Nervously, to himself)* The wretched woman! The wretched woman!

IVANOVICH: *(Amiably)* I heard your playing, Ekaterina Ivanova. In fact, the servants were listening to it on the radio.

EKATERINA: Servants? You have those, do you?

IVANOVICH: It was very beautiful.

EKATERINA: What was?

IVANOVICH: Your playing. I'd like to have a record of it to listen to.

EKATERINA: Well, what else would you do with it? Eat your dinner off it? Mind you, when I lend some of mine out to friends they . . .

(Boris shudders)

IVANOVICH: Quite so. Anyway, if you would be so kind, comrade?

EKATERINA: It's very late and I'm very tired. It's really unreasonable of you, Ivan Ivanovich.

IVANOVICH: *(To Boris)* She says I'm being unreasonable.

BORIS: *(Shocked)* Certainly not, sir. You are kindness itself.

IVANOVICH: *(Unconvinced. To Ekaterina)* Madam, I don't think you realise who you're talking to.

EKATERINA: Oh, but I do, Ivan Ivanovich. I certainly do. And what's more, every night I pray for your dark and dismal soul.

BORIS: *(Drops a tray of drinks)* Oh my word! My word! Heavens! We'll all be for the chop. Does she know what she's saying? She's gone crazy!

IVANOVICH: I thank you for praying for my soul. Now will you make the record?

EKATERINA: Ask me again. Nicely.

IVANOVICH: Would you please make the record, dearest comrade?

EKATERINA: Pardon?

IVANOVICH: Gracious lady, I would be deeply indebted if you would be so kind . . .

EKATERINA: It's getting better. I'll have to think about it. *(Long silence)* Very well. I'll do it. But on one condition . . .

IVANOVICH: Of course! Of course! Name it.

(Ekaterina speaks softly, inaudibly into the phone)

BORIS: *(To audience)* They were working on it all through the night. I said to Ivan Ivanovich, if she's being difficult, get someone else. No, he says. It *has* to be her. Her playing. No one else.

Then he asks me again if Mozart was a genius. Very strange. Not like him. Not like him at all. In fact, he's been strange ever since. Well anyway, she agreed to do it. Face as black as thunder all through the recording, apparently. Says I've already given one performance tonight, so why should I go through it all again for some silly old fool who wants his own record? There were gasps all round the auditorium. The orchestra begged her. Said it was more than their lives were worth. To which she says one life from you is worth a thousand silly old Ivanoviches. More gasps. Anyway, they do the recording, rush it off to the factory, work flat out and here it is.

(Holds up record gingerly, as if it were some kind of host. A bell rings)

I wonder if this is the first record to order, in history. Perhaps someone would like to look that up. And in twenty-four hours, no less. Beautiful, isn't it? The way the light catches the grooves. Like a rainbow. There are three of them.

(Holds up Record One)

First movement. Second movement. Third.

(Pauses)

I wonder why he didn't get angry with Ekaterina like he usually does. Did you hear what she said to him? I pray for . . . Well, I dropped a whole tray of drinks, I can tell you. I was half expecting my one-way ticket to . . . *(Pause)* I wonder why . . .

(Ivanovich enters)

IVANOVICH: Boris? Where's my breakfast?

BORIS: But it's five o'clock, sir.

IVANOVICH: Five o'clock?

BORIS: In the afternoon.

IVANOVICH: Good lord! I've been asleep for hours.

BORIS: Yes, sir.

IVANOVICH: Can't remember any of my dreams.

BORIS: Yes, sir. You've certainly slept well.

IVANOVICH: Must be that bloody woman. Tired me out. I'm not used to such behaviour, you know. It's quite disconcerting. Did you hear what she said?

BORIS: I tried not to.

IVANOVICH: But you *did* hear? *(Boris nods)* Says she prays every night for my black soul. She must be the only one who does. Unless *you* do and you're not telling me.

BORIS: No, sir. No.

IVANOVICH: Well, I suppose I've missed breakfast so I'll go straight into supper. Have them bring it up to me. I don't want to see anyone today.

BORIS: Your record, sir. It's come.

IVANOVICH: *(Nonchalantly)* Good. I'll listen to it after supper.

(Attendants bring Ivan's supper. Someone tests the food. Ivan eats slowly, thoughtfully. They bring his rocking-chair. They leave him. They take away some dishes. He sits for a moment, then goes to put on the music. Entire slow movement of Piano Concerto no. 23. Sits with back to audience. Rocks slightly from time to time. Just towards the end, Ivan slumps back in chair. Record hisses on groove. After a while Boris hears the noise and comes scuttling in)

BORIS: Did you enjoy that, sir? I'll take it off. It's not good for the needle, apparently. Wears it out. Did you want the other one?

> *(Boris turns round. Sees Ivan slumped. Stops. Hesitates. Goes slowly forward, tentatively)*

   Sir?
> *(He shakes the chair gently)*
   Sir?
> *(Steps back for a moment, then realises.)*

   The record's finished, sir. It's finished.

> *(Then, panic-stricken)*

   Sir? What do you want me to do?

SUPERIOR BARGAINS

CAST LIST

Danny—A Sales Assistant

Joe—A Sales Assistant

Cindy—A Sales Assistant

Mr. Smythe—Supervisor

First Nun

Second Nun

French Nun

(The action takes place in one continuous scene)

(Inside a large department store. Danny, Joe, Cindy and Mr. Smythe. Danny is walking up and down)

DANNY: Aren't you just a little bit nervous?

JOE: Nervous? No more than usual. Why?

DANNY: Well, about the opening.

JOE: I'm sure it'll be fine. I was more nervous last night. So much so, that me and Zoe decided to christen the kitchen table.

DANNY: Christen? What do you mean?

JOE: I'll explain it to you later. *(Cindy enters)*

CINDY: Hi, boys.

DANNY & JOE: Hi, Cindy.

CINDY: It's a daft idea this night opening. I'm going to have problems keeping awake tonight.

JOE: No difference there, I see.

CINDY: Comical, I'm sure. But why do they have to open a new store at *midnight?* What's wrong with during the day? It seems a silly idea.

DANNY: It's a time for night owls and wolves. *(He makes a wolf call)* Aruuu!

CINDY: *(Slaps him gently)* Stop it!

DANNY: Did you see that? That's sexual molestation and harassment, that is.

CINDY: You wouldn't know sexual harassment if it came up and poked you in the eye. Would he, Joe?

JOE: I'm saying nothing.

DANNY: Aruuu!

JOE: Stop it, Danny!

DANNY: If I can scare the customers off, then maybe we can go home early. What time are we on till, anyway?

CINDY: I'm off at five thirty. I've got my paper round to do.

DANNY & JOE: Paper round?

CINDY: It's for my uncle. He's got a bad back. I'm doing it till he gets better. He doesn't want to lose it, you see. *(Enter Mr. Smythe)*

SMYTHE: And very commendable it is too, Cindy. Well done. If all staff at Pantop Perkins showed the same devotion, well think where we'd be . . . .

JOE: Devotion?

SMYTHE: That's what I said. And while your uncle's indisposed, we're more than happy to accommodate you, Cindy.

DANNY: Indisposed? She's going home for a shag, more like!

SMYTHE: *(Sternly)* How rude! That will do, Danny. There's no call for that kind of vulgarity.

DANNY: I was merely making a point. Anyway, there's always time for a shag. Just ask Joe. He christened his kitchen table last night.

JOE: *(Angrily)* I thought you didn't . . .

SMYTHE: Oh dear! I hope it wasn't one of ours. Did it stand up to . . . ?

JOE: Don't worry, Mr. S. It didn't let us down, if that's what you're thinking. Which is more than can be said for Superposture Beds.

SMYTHE: Thankfully that product has been withdrawn. All kinds of accidents. As a matter of fact, I don't know what it is with you two, but the conversation always seems to descend to coarseness when you're around.

DANNY: It's too much sitting, that's what it is.

SMYTHE: Pardon? I'm afraid you've lost me there.

JOE: He's right. It's sitting.

SMYTHE: I fail to see . . .

JOE: I got a leaflet when I was in Oxford Street once. The Protein Wisdom Group.

SMYTHE: The Protein Wisdom Group? Is that a variation of the Atkins diet?

JOE: Hardly, sir. It has a motto. 'Less lust from fewer proteins'.

SMYTHE: Joseph, you're at it again.

JOE: I'm quoting, sir. 'Egg, meat, fish, bird. And sitting'.

SMYTHE: Sitting?

JOE: Yes, sitting. It was quite an informative book. I bought it for a number of friends of mine as I thought they were in need of it.

SMYTHE: And what is the correlation between proteins and sitting?

JOE: Well, sitting is the problem, apparently. Makes you, you know, if you have too many proteins . . .

DANNY: Randy. That's what he's trying to say. Randy.

SMYTHE: Yes, thank you. I'm well aware of the definition.

JOE: That's why there's so much sex in the office.

SMYTHE: *(Anxiously) Which* office?

JOE: I wasn't meaning any particular one. Just in general.

SMYTHE: Oh dear. This is what I mean. Every time there's a conversation it comes down to this. Remember there are ladies present.

DANNY: *(Incredulously)* Ladies?

CINDY: He means me you fool!

JOE: I can only see one.

SMYTHE: I was speaking figuratively.

DANNY: I bet you were.

SMYTHE: Now enough of this!

DANNY: What time are we on till?

SMYTHE: Half past eight. Now, Danny, did you put that advert out?

DANNY: About the opening times?

SMYTHE: Yes. The press release.

DANNY: I did, Mr. Smythe.

SMYTHE: Good. I can only say that I'm glad I vetted it.

DANNY: Why's that, Mr. S.

SMYTHE: Your slogan. 'Perkins, the store for Mums on Top' was not entirely . . . appropriate.

DANNY: It wasn't?

SMYTHE: No. It was unfortunately open to misinterpretation.

CINDY: Oh dear!

DANNY: And I couldn't spell that other word you gave me.

SMYTHE: Ah yes. Superior. Ha! Ha!

CINDY: It's all right, Mr. Smythe. I helped him.

SMYTHE:	Well, thank you, Cindy. You're an inspiration and a credit to us all.
JOE:	An inspiration of what, Mr. S?
SMYTHE:	She helps out family and colleagues alike.
CINDY:	You what, Mr. Smythe? We don't have any animals, I'm afraid.
SMYTHE:	Sorry, dear. I'm not with you.
CINDY:	*(Realising)* Oh, I'm sorry too. I thought you said collies.
JOE:	So why do we have to open the new store at midnight?
SMYTHE:	It's obvious. It's a special occasion. A unique opportunity. Thanks to Danny's press release and the publicity it'll generate, I expect we'll be inundated.
CINDY:	But who goes shopping in the middle of the night?
SMYTHE:	The Americans for one.
DANNY:	For one what?
SMYTHE:	*(Ignoring him)* When I was in Los Angeles . . . .
JOE:	Here we go again.
SMYTHE:	A little respect and politeness, please!
DANNY:	Cindy's right. Who would go shopping for a sofa at two o'clock in the morning?
CINDY:	That's right. There'd be no buses.
SMYTHE:	*(Puzzled)* Well, plenty of people would. My wife, for one.
DANNY:	*(Titters)* Shouldn't she be doing other things at two o'clock in the morning?
SMYTHE:	I shan't speak to you again! *(Pauses for breath)* Now, if we can all stop being silly for a moment.
CINDY:	But *you* weren't being silly, Mr. Smythe.

SMYTHE: No, I *wasn't*. Thank you, Cindy.

CINDY: I'm all yours, Mr. Smythe.

JOE: Brownhooter!

DANNY: Grovelbottom!

CINDY: Brown what?

SMYTHE: Stop it, you two! Now, I'm pleased to tell you that Mrs. Deborah Waddle is going to be in charge of the new staff canteen.

DANNY: I hope it's better than the last one.

CINDY: Debbie? You mean Debbie from the High Street Caff?

SMYTHE: The very same. Mrs. Waddle it is.

JOE: There's something wrong with that sentence?

SMYTHE: Pardon?

JOE: Shouldn't it be 'it is Mrs. Waddle'?

SMYTHE: You silly, uncouth youth. It's an emphatic inversion?

DANNY: Does your wife know about this?

SMYTHE: What's my wife got to do with it? Kindly leave her out, please!

DANNY: About these inversions!

SMYTHE: Silence! Any more and I'll have you carpeted! *(Danny sniggers)* Now let me tell you about Deborah. She has decided to join our partnership to further her standards of excellent catering.

CINDY: That's not what she told *me*, Mr. Smythe. She said it was because of the break-ins.

SMYTHE: Break-ins?

CINDY: Yes. Got right fed up she did. Put a notice in the window. No cash left overnight. That's because Vera, who helps her, goes to the bank at three. She even left the till open. On display! But the buggers still broke in. It was the sandwiches they were after.

SMYTHE: That's terrible. Poor Deborah!

CINDY: They started eating the sandwiches *and* cooking food in the kitchen.

SMYTHE: The poor woman!

CINDY: One day she came in and they'd left the washing up. That was the final straw! It wouldn't have been so bad but they'd pinched all the washing up liquid, too.

JOE: Shocking, sir, isn't it? The *times* we live in!

SMYTHE: Well that's not what I was told. They said she was looking forward to forging a unique partnership.

JOE: It's your lucky day then, sir, isn't it?

SMYTHE: Well, if what you say is true, Cindy, we shall give Mrs. Waddle our complete support.

DANNY: Bang on, sir!

(Smythe gives Danny a dirty look.)

DANNY: I mean, I agree, sir.

SMYTHE: Thank you, Daniel. You know, I have to say, when I came in at seven o'clock this evening and walked along the aisles of the store, I couldn't help experiencing a feeling of pride. There was a buzz of nervous expectancy.
            A hum.

JOE: That'll be the lights, sir. They play havoc with my eyes. It makes me think I'm in a department store. *(Giggles)*

SMYTHE: No, Joseph. It was the sensation of something *about* to happen. The aisles and carpets were beautifully clean. Pristine, in fact. The sofas, immaculate. Inviting, almost.

DANNY: *(Yawns)* I could do with a sofa right now. A bit of shut-eye.

SMYTHE: The colours were beautiful in their combinations. Dazzling yet tasteful. And the tables with their dripping scent of polish and beeswax.

CINDY: They'll be snapped up, I'm sure.

SMYTHE: Cindy?

CINDY: Well, they're part of the bargain range.

SMYTHE: Indeed they are. We're trading at highly competitive prices!

CINDY: No, no, Mr. Smythe. They're the super bargains. First hundred customers and all that.

JOE: I still think it's a funny time to open.

SMYTHE: Nonsense. I think I already mentioned America to you.

JOE: You did, sir. And what a backward, bloody place it is too!

SMYTHE: You've lost me.

DANNY: I don't think so. More's the pity!

SMYTHE: Why do you say backward, Joseph?

JOE: Because the poor sods only get two weeks' holiday a year! Can you imagine it?

DANNY: It's disgusting!

CINDY: Sad.

JOE: It's a bloody scandal. They should take it to the Court of Human Rights!

SMYTHE: I don't think we'll start involving ourselves in politics.

CINDY: It always makes me cry.

SMYTHE: Two weeks is more than sufficient. It's only a matter of time before *we* adopt such practices. Now, come along everyone. We need to press on. To focus on our work. I'm off for a cup of tea and I suggest you do the same. To refresh us for the battle ahead. *(Pleased with his own joke)* Now, Daniel, if you're feeling sleepy, what about a nice strong cup of coffee?

JOE: It gives him palpitations, Mr. Smythe. Very unwise. He might start biting the carpet.

SMYTHE: I needn't remind you that all breakages must be paid for, in line with company policy. *(Looks at his watch)* Very well, we'll meet again in twenty minutes.

(Exit Mr. Smythe)

JOE: Pompous plonker!

CINDY: He's just doing his job. What's wrong with that?

JOE: Inflated arse!

CINDY: *(Suddenly shrieks)* Oh my, what was that?

DANNY: What was what?

CINDY: *(Trembling)* I saw something. Something out there. In the car park.

JOE: What did you see, Cindy?

CINDY: A shape. I saw a black shape. It looked terrible.

DANNY: It's okay, Cindy. You've been listening to Mr. Smythe rabbiting on. It's enough to give anyone hallucinations.

CINDY:	I *wasn't* hallucinating. I definitely saw something.
JOE:	What was it, Cind?
CINDY:	I told you, a dark, mysterious shape.
JOE:	A large black shape or a little black shape?
CINDY:	*(Anxiously)* I don't know. *(Sits down)* Maybe it was nothing. Perhaps it was a trick of the light. Probably me just feeling tired. It's a long night and then I've got the paper round to do. *(Pause)* I think I'll just go to the loo.

(She exits)

DANNY:	Yeah, I need to go too. It's all the excitement. *(He glances out of the window. Momentarily freezes)* Joe! Cindy ain't kidding! I saw something out there an' all.
JOE:	Where?
DANNY:	To the left of the outside building. It was scurrying like a demon. Look! There goes another one.
JOE:	*(Peers out of the window)* I can't see anything.
DANNY:	It looks like a giant bird. A crow or something, only bigger.
JOE:	I think I can see something. It's black with a small white ring at the top . . .
DANNY:	That's it! That's what we saw!
JOE:	There are loads of them. It's like a flock of giant penguins.
DANNY:	Penguins? You're joking! *(Pause)* This is weird.
JOE:	You don't think it's some kind of advertising stunt? One of Mr. S's odd gimmicks.

DANNY: Nah. What would they be advertising, anyway? Look! They're all milling around. There's hundreds of 'em. They're banging on the windows. *(Sounds of banging and shouting can be heard)*

JOE: Quick! Call Mr. S. He'll know what to do.

VOICE: *(On Loudspeaker)* All staff in position, please. Doors are about to open . . . Store opening in one minute. *(Chimes of Big Ben on radio)*

RADIO ANNOUNCER: It's midnight. Here is the news with . . .

(More crashes and shouts. Mr. Smythe rushes in with Cindy)

SMYTHE: I can't believe it! It's quite extraordinary! I've never seen anything like it.

CINDY: I was *right*, wasn't I? I *did* see something.

JOE: She did. A flock of giant bloody penguins.

CINDY: That mysterious dark shape in the staff car park.

SMYTHE: That mysterious shape was a nun!

DANNY, CINDY & JOE: A nun?

SMYTHE: Yes. The store is full of them. Thousands of them.

JOE: But what would nuns be doing in a place like this? There must be some mistake. Maybe it's a coach party. That's it. They're on the way back from Skeggy or something and they've stopped off for a drink.

SMYTHE:	Buffoon! Nuns do not go to Skegness! Nor do nuns take holidays! No, I fear something is very wrong. Daniel, what did you *put* in that advert?
DANNY:	*(Anxiously)* Me, Mr. Smythe?
SMYTHE:	Yes, you, sir!
DANNY:	Only what you told me to.
SMYTHE:	Nothing else?
DANNY:	No. Why would I? I had enough problems with that word you gave me.
SMYTHE:	Refresh my memory. What did you write exactly?
DANNY:	Exactly? Er, well, let me see. Pantop Perkins—Special Opening—Everything you need for a Mother Superior.
SMYTHE:	*(Puts head in hands)* Arggh! I don't believe it!
DANNY:	Believe what?
SMYTHE:	You stupid boy!
DANNY:	Come on, Mr. S, I didn't mean . . .
CINDY:	*(Grabs Smythe's hand)* Think calmness. Think blood pressure . . .
SMYTHE:	You fool! You dolt! You pineapple-brain! You've just invited a flock of nuns to the first night opening!
JOE:	I *wasn't* wrong, then.
SMYTHE:	Wrong what?
CINDY:	*I* saw them first. They were sneaking up around the building.
JOE:	In a highly precise and tactical operation.
DANNY:	All those mysterious penguin shapes . . .
JOE:	So, the store's full of them? What's wrong with that?

SMYTHE: What's wrong? Have you been out there? It's mayhem. Chaos.

(They hear a crash. Voices of nuns. Three nuns fall onto the stage)

NUN 1:   That bed's mine, you bastard! I saw it first!

NUN 2:   It's mine, I tell you. Get your thieving hands off!

FRENCH NUN: 'Ow dare you! Zis is mine. All mine!

NUN 1:   You've got a nerve, sister. You're not even local.

FRENCH NUN: So what's, flabbyface. I come all ze way from Belgium. I see zis notice. C'est fantastique, n'est-ce pas?

NUN 2:   If either of you doesn't get their mits off this, so help me, I'll . . .

(They spill further onto the stage. More brawling.)

SMYTHE: *(Remonstrating and deeply shocked)* Ladies! Ladies! This is no way to carry on. I'm sure we can resolve this.

(Mr. Smythe is knocked to the floor in the ensuing brawl. He manages to get up with the help of Danny. Shrieks and bonks throughout the store)

            They're everywhere! The whole store! And the language! I've never heard such . . . before!

JOE: That'll be Latin, I expect.

SMYTHE: *(Angrily)* I see. You're an expert, then? I can assure you that's not Latin! It's most definitely Anglo-Saxon.

CINDY: Is it? Oh dear, what can we do, then?

NUN 1:   Give it here, you shameless, brazen hussy!

NUN 2:   Yes, hands off, you fish-faced Flem . . .

FRENCH NUN: Ah, non alors! Zat is ze last straw. Zat break ze pig's trotters. *(Takes a swing at Nun 2)* I am no Flem. I am a Wally from ze Frenssh part.

SMYTHE: It's turning ugly.

ALL NUNS: There's no need to be personal!

SMYTHE: It's a riot! Full scale chaos!

CINDY: What are you going to do, Mr. Smythe?

SMYTHE: What I should have done earlier. Call the police.

NUN 2:   Ah sure, that's a waste of time, brother. There'll be nobody there.

SMYTHE: How can you know that, sister?

NUN 2:   Half the buggers'll be down the Dog and Duck. It's the karaoke night. The other half'll be raiding Sister Mathilda's.

SMYTHE: Sister Mathilda's? What is that?

DANNY :   It sounds like a night club or something.

SMYTHE: Don't be disrespectful, Danny. Remember whom we're in the presence of.

DANNY: Oh, yes, I can see. *(Dodges flying object)*

NUN 2:   It's Sister Mathilda's cannabis convention. When I say 'raiding', it's usually a 50/50 split between Sister Matty and the old Bill. The lads put something in the charity box sometimes. You should also try her cakes. Absolutely delicious!

(Exit nuns)

SMYTHE: What are we to do if the police won't help? The new store'll be ruined. I've never seen such aggression, such hostility!

DANNY: You don't believe all that nonsense she's just been spinning you?

SMYTHE: I have no reason to doubt her word.

JOE: It's all those pent up feelings, sir. That's why there's so much agro. All those years of being good. It's *bound* to take its toll.

SMYTHE: It's that idiot, Daniel! It's all *his* doing!

JOE: Pardon me, sir, but it's that word of yours, the 'superior', that's caused all this.

SMYTHE: By entrusting it to a pea-brain! Yes, of *course,* it has!

CINDY: Listen! Why don't you all stop squabbling for a minute? Does it matter now whose fault it is? We have to deal with the problem as it stands.

(There is a staggered silence)

JOE: Well, yes. Cindy's right.

CINDY: I'm trying to think of a way round this.

DANNY: Atta girl, Cindy!

CINDY: It's coming back to me.

JOE: What is?

CINDY: Well, when my granddad used to have trouble with nuns, he always dialled a certain number.

SMYTHE: *(Skeptically)* I don't believe it. What trouble did he have?

CINDY: The nuns used to take a short cut through his allotment on Sundays sometimes. It was usually on the way back from the pub.

SMYTHE: Shocking!

CINDY: Well, the Horse and Groom was right opposite the church. That's why. A sort of perennial temptation. Anyway, it couldn't be helped. You see, he was a bit of a glamour boy in his youth. He'd come out of that potting shed and find himself surrounded by them.

SMYTHE: So, what did he do, then? What was that number, Cindy?

CINDY: I'm trying to think, Mr. Smythe. It's all a bit of a blur.

SMYTHE: Think quickly, Cindy! Think!

CINDY: Let me try and picture it. There's the shed. The watering can. The hosepipe on the left. Or was it on the right? There was a rhubarb patch just outside the door.

SMYTHE: Cindy! This is no time for elaborate descriptions. The store's fate lies in the balance!

CINDY: I know, I know, Mr. Smythe, but it's important that I get this right.

JOE: Would a piece of cake aid your memory?

CINDY: *(Deliberating)* You know, Joe, I think it would.

SMYTHE: Streuth!

JOE: You may think this silly, Mr. Smythe, but the choice of cake can be very important.

SMYTHE: *(Coldly)* So it would seem. Very well, send for the cake list.

JOE: No, it's too dangerous out there. *(Noise of distant shrieks and shouts)* Let me see if the lines are still working. *(Lifts up phone)* Yes, they are. We can ring down. It's safer. *(Dials number)* Hello? Yes. Who is that? Brenda? Okay. I need to know what cakes you've got today. Okay. *(To Smythe and Cindy)* She's just going to find her glasses. It works better with them on. *(More crashes and shrieks)* Right. Okay. Yes. Victoria Sponge. Two kinds of filling. Lemon Drizzle Cake. Aunty Sally's Jam Roly Poly. Carrot Cake soaked in rum—sounds delicious. Coffee and Walnut.

CINDY: Would you mind repeating that, Joe?

SMYTHE*:*   *(Groans deeply)* Tell me it's not true!

CINDY: *(Looking at him anxiously)* Well, I *could* try a bit of both . . .

SMYTHE: A bit of both? A bit of both? Cindy, the store is collapsing all around us and here you are deliberating about cakes.

CINDY: *(Ignores him)* Victoria Sponge and Lemon Dribble, please.

DANNY: Yeah. Victoria Sponge and Lemon. Always nice. I'll have a piece of the Coffee and Walnut.

SMYTHE: Good grief, man!

DANNY: Like she says, man, you can't rush these things.

JOE: Particularly as memory is such a changeable commodity.

SMYTHE: *As* she says.

DANNY: As she says what?

SMYTHE: You can't say 'like'. You have to say 'as'.

DANNY: That's ridiculous.

SMYTHE: I wasn't the one ordering the cake!

JOE: *(To Danny)* It doesn't matter, mate. Humour him. Keep him distracted. And don't let him wander off. It's *dangerous* out there.

(Helmeted courier brings tray of cakes.)

COURIER: Here you are, lads. It was touch and go. They nearly got snaffled on the way.

JOE: How are things on the other floors?

COURIER: I didn't stop to look. But some of the staff was being taken away in lorries. At least, that's what I heard. You could hear the noise. Terrible, it was.

JOE: Did you find out anything else?

COURIER   Well, if you're looking for a ringleader, I think it might be that Sister Philomena. Her organizational powers are phenomenal.

CINDY: *(Samples both cakes)* Mm! Not bad. *(Pause)* That's it! Of course! How could I have been so stupid? That's it! Dial a Bishop!

ALL: Pardon?

CINDY: That's what granddad used to do. Whenever he had problems with nuns, he used to call the Dial a Bishop service.

SMYTHE: Dial a Bishop? Are you sure? I've never heard of it!

CINDY: Well, you've probably never had an allotment, Mr. Smythe. Anyway, whenever the nuns got a bit out of hand, you know, Sunday lunchtimes, he used to ring it. Things soon got back to normal, thanks to the bishop.

SMYTHE: *(Shakes his head)* It hardly seems possible.

JOE: *(To Mr. Smythe)* We can't afford to be skeptical, sir. Especially when you consider what's at stake.

SMYTHE: I know, I know. I was just a little taken aback, that's all.

JOE: We've got to try it. If the pigs are off their faces on Mathilda's cup cakes, it's our only chance.

SMYTHE: But how do you *know* she makes cup cakes? And I do wish you wouldn't use those terms of familiarity, Joe. It's the *police!*

JOE: All right, it's the police what's off their faces.

SMYTHE: And besides, my aunt once had a pig called Emily. She was a truly delightful creature. Extremely sensitive.

JOE: All right, all right! The number!

SMYTHE: *(Picks up phone)* Yes, please. Dial a Bishop! It's urgent!

CINDY: I'm so glad to have been of help. I really needed that cake.

JOE: It's quite strange the associations you can get with things. I got nothing out of that Coffee and Walnut.

CINDY: It looked a bit bland, actually.

JOE: What about the Lemon Drizzle?

CINDY: Not bad, but still a little sweet. These shop ones are. I could have done with much more lemon.

SMYTHE: *(Waves arms)* Quiet, everyone! I've got through!

VOICE of BISHOP: Bishop Snoad here.

SMYTHE: My Lord Bishop!

BISHOP: I am the *duty* bishop. How can I be of assistance?

SMYTHE: We are in dire straits, my Lord.

BISHOP: Life's meandering path is full of problems. I'm listening to you, my child.

SMYTHE: My Lord, our store, the newly opened one on Selsey Marsh, is in the hands of a delinquent horde of invaders. Of rampant nuns, no less.

BISHOP: But not at *this* hour, surely?

SMYTHE: The store's future is at stake!

BISHOP: But tell me, my child, are they Catholic or Anglican nuns?

SMYTHE: I'm sorry, bishop. What do you mean?

BISHOP: What I said. Are they Anglican or Catholic nuns?

SMYTHE: Is it important?

BISHOP: Extremely. We need to establish exactly where the nuns emanate from.

SMYTHE: But how can I tell? Should I just go and ask? It's too dangerous out there. They're lobbing settees from the windows and into waiting lorries.

BISHOP: Dear me! Well, it's quite easy. There's usually a logo or insignia at the back of the habit.

SMYTHE: I see. And what are these . . . . ?

CINDY: *(To Danny)* We need to identify them first.

SMYTHE: Yes, thank you, Cindy. Go quickly and have a look. Tell me what you see. But be careful.

CINDY: Very well, Mr. Smythe. But wouldn't it be better if *you* went?

SMYTHE: No, no, Cindy! We haven't time. Hurry!

(More sounds of brawling and shouting)

Interlude (Song)

CINDY:	*(Returns)* I've found out, Mr. S.
SMYTHE:	Well done, girl
CINDY	*(Speaks to Bishop)* They are Catholic nuns, my Lord.
BISHOP:	Shameful! Are they really? Well, that falls within my jurisdiction, luckily. If they were of the other persuasion, then you would have to contact Bishop Egremont. He's a splendid fellow, though. You'd have no problems with him. Anyway, I shall come and talk to the wayward sisters. I may even *know* some of the miscreants. A good talking to sometimes works wonders. I'll be over straight away.
SMYTHE:	We are indebted to you, your Grace. *(To Danny)* You see where your clumsy wording has got us!
JOE:	Leave it out, Mr. S. We need to work together. Present a united front for when the bishop comes. It won't give a good impression if we're squabbling and fighting amongst ourselves. That sort of behaviour is reserved for the customers downstairs.
SMYTHE:	How long will it take him to get here, do you think?
CINDY:	My granddad always said it was a very prompt service. He never had any complaints about it.
SMYTHE:	Yes, but what time difference are we talking here? I mean, how long ago? What with all these cuts in services . . . Agencies, privatizations, putting out to tender . . . Those kinds of things.
CINDY:	*(Worried)* Oh dear, I hadn't thought of that. You mean the bishop might be privatised?
JOE:	It's more than likely.

CINDY: Oh, I can't follow all this. Why can't they leave things alone? I'm sure they were fine the way they were.

JOE: Don't worry. I'm certain he'll be here soon.

DANNY: Well, that could mean *anything*. When P.C. Plod says right away, it's any time next week. And then along comes some spotty 'Herbert who just gives you a list of telephone numbers.

JOE: Maybe we should make an announcement. You know, over the loudspeakers.

CINDY: To say what?

JOE: That reinforcements are on their way.

SMYTHE: That's right. We could exaggerate it a bit.

JOE: Yeah, Cindy. Just say a gaggle of bishops are approaching the store now.

CINDY: Are they likely to believe that?

SMYTHE: I'm not so sure. And what about that word gaggle? It sounds a bit disrespectful for bishops. Now what's the collective noun? Er . . . Let me see. Bench! Yes, that's it. A bench of bishops. Joe, get on the Tannoy right away!

JOE: I think Danny has a better voice for it. How about it, Danny?

DANNY: It's the least I can do, Mr. Smythe. *(Picks up microphone)* All right, all right. All you nuns out there. Listen! What I have to say is this. A bench of bishops is on its way to the store this very minute. They're coming to er . . .

SMYTHE: You make it sound like they're going shopping, too. What you *should* say is the bishops are coming to restore a sense of order and decency. Not to mention decorum.

DANNY: I can't say that.

SMYTHE: Why ever not?

DANNY: Well it sounds silly, dunnit?

SMYTHE: Just say it! *Say* it, for pity's sake!

DANNY: *(To Joe)* I've got a much better idea. *(Speaks into mike. Largely incoherent)*

SMYTHE: *(Weeps)* It's too much!

CINDY: *(Consoles Mr. Smythe)* Don't cry! Don't cry, Mr. Smythe! We're all here for you, aren't we, Joe?

JOE: That's right.

SMYTHE: It's just the disappointment, you understand. I was *so* looking forward to this day. In my mind I'd been going through all the preparations, the last minute details. Everybody's worked so hard. I would never have imagined that it would all be undone by an unruly herd of nuns.

JOE: It's the times we live in. I often blame the parents.

SMYTHE: And now everything's being trampled underfoot. The spirit of consumerism has been unleashed even in the nunneries and whose members, held back and denied for so long, have finally given way to their baser instincts. And all because of *one* silly mistake!

JOE: I know, Mr. S. That's the essence of tragedy really?

CINDY: What is?

JOE: Wording is so important nowadays; using the right word. But Danny didn't mean any harm. He wasn't to know. It was just a slight slip. Any one of us could have made it.

DANNY: Listen, everyone.

CINDY: Listen to what?

DANNY: Can you hear? The store's beginning to empty. I'm sure of it. I'll go and look. *(Exit Danny)*

CINDY: It's certainly got a lot quieter, Dan.

JOE: Bravo, Danny boy!

CINDY: *(Looks out of the window)* They're leaving. They're putting the goods into lorries and driving off.

JOE: By the time the bishop comes, they may all be gone.

CINDY: Typical!

SMYTHE: That's a point. We don't want to look foolish in front of the bishop.

JOE: May I make a suggestion, sir?

SMYTHE: By all means.

JOE: Send Danny out with his camera. There's bound to be a few stragglers left. You know, take a few piccies as evidence.

DANNY: *(Returns)* They've all gone.

CINDY: You're a hero, Dan. I'm so proud of you.

JOE: What did you tell them?

DANNY: Me? Nothing really. I told them about the bishop and . . . .

JOE: And?

DANNY: They just ignored me. Carried on fighting. It was only when I said there was a massive carpet sale down the road that they all ran out of the building.

SMYTHE: Good heavens!

JOE: Smart work, Danny. You're not as daft as you look.

DANNY: Thanks, Joe.

CINDY: What's that you've got there?

DANNY: A video. I found it on the floor in the furniture department.

CINDY: I didn't know we sold videos.

JOE: Maybe someone dropped it. Stick it on, then. We've got a few minutes before the bishop comes.

CINDY: *(To Mr. Smythe)* Danny's saved our bacon, Mr. Smythe. It was his cleverness that saved us. Mention of the bishop had no effect but when he said there was a carpet sale . . . .

SMYTHE: Maybe so, Cindy, but it was *Danny* who started all this.

CINDY: And he's *sorted* it. Don't be too hard on him. He's a lovely lad, really.

SMYTHE: I shall have to think about this.

VOICE of MICHAEL WOOD: *(From the video)* And that was only the beginning of the story . . .

SMYTHE: Isn't that the history man, Michael Wood?

JOE: It could be. Tall, skinny bloke?

VOICE: *(Continues)* The shopping malls of today are the equivalents of our bygone medieval cathedrals. We no longer build these places but instead under these vast new canopies of glass . . .

SMYTHE: I used to love those programmes

JOE: I can hear a car outside. *(Sound of car horn tooting)*

CINDY: That'll be His Lordship.

SMYTHE: Get the cakes ready, Cindy. We may need to lay on a good spread. And rewind the video. He might like to watch it.

(Adjusts his tie and smoothes down his hair)

Just a minute. We're coming, my Lord. We're coming!

Edwards Brothers, Inc.
Thorofare, NJ USA
November 16, 2011